OCT 30 1993

NOV 16 1993
DEC - 6 1993

MAR 21 1994

SEP 27 1994
NOV - 7 1994

FEB 25 1995
MAR 17 1995

APR - 3 1995
JUN 16 1995

OCT - 2 1995

NOV 25 1995
MAR - 9 1996

MAY 12 1996
SEP 24 1996

OCT 19 1996
DEC 23 1997

75-00226

970.3 Navajo history. Written under the direction
N   of the Navajo Curriculum Center, Rough Rock
v.1   Demonstration School, Chinle, Arizona
         Editor: Ethelou Yazzie. Illustrator: Andy
MAY - 5 19Tsihnahjinnie. Photographer: Martin Hoff-
         man. Navajo Community College Pr.,
         1971-
         v illus.

SAN MATEO PUBLIC LIBRARY
SAN MATEO, CALIF.

1. Navaho Indians- Religion and mythology
2. Navaho Indians- Hist. I. Yazzie, Ethelou,
ed. II. Navajo Curriculum Center

70-167801   12/74 1200

NAVAJO HISTORY

DEDICATED...

To the Navajo People

NAVAJO HISTORY

Volume 1

Written Under
The Direction of   The Navajo Curriculum Center
Rough Rock Demonstration School
Chinle, Arizona 86503

Editor   Ethelou Yazzie

Illustrator   Andy Tsihnahjinnie

Photographer   Martin Hoffman

Publisher   Navajo Community College Press
Many Farms, Arizona 86503

1971

Copyright © 1971

By

Navajo Curriculum Center

Rough Rock Demonstration School

Chinle, Arizona 86503

ALL RIGHTS RESERVED,
INCLUDING THE RIGHT TO REPRODUCE THIS BOOK
OR PARTS THEREOF IN ANY FORM

International Standard Book Number 0-912586-11-7

Library of Congress Catalog Card Number 70-167802

FIRST EDITION

Printed in the United States of America

CONTENTS

ACKNOWLEDGMENTS 6

Chapter   Page

1. THE FIRST WORLD — THE BLACK WORLD 9

2. THE SECOND WORLD — THE BLUE WORLD 11

3. THE THIRD WORLD — THE YELLOW WORLD 13

4. THE FOURTH WORLD — THE GLITTERING WORLD..... 17

5. ASDZĄ́Ą́ NÁDLEEHÉ (CHANGING WOMAN) 47

6. KILLING THE MONSTERS 59

7. ORIGIN OF THE CLANS 74

8. DIVISION OF THE PEOPLE........................ 83

GLOSSARY.. 87

    It should be emphasized that there are many different versions of the origin of the Navajos and of the accounts of the various underworlds. Little agreement exists regarding the exact number of the previous worlds or of the events which occurred in each; and there is disagreement as to the colors assigned to those various worlds. Nevertheless, there is basic accord concerning the major events of the Tribe's prehistory; and it is said that the beauty of the stories of the Navajos' creation and origin surely equals the beauty contained in Genesis.

ACKNOWLEDGMENTS

WITH THE COMPLETION of this volume of Navajo tribal prehistory, it is particularly appropriate to consider the reason for its being: to present, for the first time, a statement of Navajo prehistory for the use of our students and others who may be interested in the earliest times as seen from the Navajo viewpoint.

Much is said currently about the need for cultural pride, and we would not detract from such statements; but, at the Rough Rock Demonstration School, we have found it easier said than done when the matter of actually teaching in the area of Navajo culture is attempted. The paucity of materials not only hinders, but provides an excuse for not even attempting, such instruction. This book has been produced to help alleviate the lack.

For three years the Rough Rock School Board has labored supervising the creation of this work, which is Volume I (unrecorded history) of a series of two. [Volume II will consider recorded history.] Although completion of the task at times seemed far away, the determination of the Board to produce such a summary for our youth was maintained, and this phase now has been completed.

Of particular importance is the fact that this is a labor brought forth by Navajo people for Navajo people. There always are many who will advise freely as to the impossibility of any proposed task. The creation of this book was no exception. Many said that it could not be done, and that, if it could, Navajo people could not do it. To such jeremiads we offer this book in refutation.

Where so many outstanding Navajo authorities on tribal prehistory were consulted, it becomes imperative to grant recognition to specific individuals.

Probably the most outstanding in terms of dedication to the project and continuing concern for the authenticity of the material was Mr. Howard Gorman. The untold hours he spent in presenting and refining material for inclusion in this work are matched only by his unfailing interest in it.

We also are deeply indebted to Mr. Scott Preston, Mr. Clyde Peshlakai, Mrs. Mary Johnson, Mr. Lee Tome, Mr. Tom Wilson, Mr. Frank Harvey, the members of the School Board at Rough Rock and the late Mr. George "Chic" Sandoval for their unquestioned expertise.

From the knowledge of the verbal literature which they supplied, this composite of Navajo prehistory was compiled. To reach consensus was no easy task, with so many slightly differing versions extant; and such was accomplished only by long periods of consultation among these Navajo scholars.

The chore of editing was done by Miss Ethelou Yazzie, while Mrs. Shirley Begay took care of the many typings of the manuscript through the various revisions leading to publication.

Finally, a note of appreciation should be given to Mr. Broderick Johnson who saw the work through the process of actual publication, to the late Mr. Martin Hoffman, to Mr. Andy Tsihnahjinnie and to Dr. Bob Roessel. Their skill is self evident; their devotion to the content of the book can be known only to those who have had the pleasure of working with them.

With this exceptional book, we feel that Rough Rock's Navajo Curriculum Center has come of age. It is a permanent part of our community's school — one in which we all take great pride.

Dillon Platero — Director
Rough Rock Demonstration School

July, 1971

Chapter 1

The First World -- The Black World

AT THE BEGINNING THERE WAS A PLACE called the Black World, where only spirit people and Holy People lived. It had four corners, and over these four corners appeared four cloud columns which were white, blue, yellow and black. The east cloud column was called Folding Dawn; the south column was Folding Sky Blue; the west one was Folding Twilight, and the north one was Folding Darkness. Coyote visited these cloud columns and changed his color to match theirs; so he is called Child of the Dawn, of the Sky Blue, of the Twilight and of the Darkness.

The First World was small in size and was much like a floating island in a sea of water mist. In the east, where the white cloud and the black cloud met, Áłtsé Hastiin (First Man) was formed. With him was formed the white corn which was perfect in shape, with kernels covering the whole ear. Doo Honoot'ínii is the name of this first seed corn, and it is also the name of the place where the white cloud and the black cloud met.

Man was not in his present shape, and the creatures living in the First World were thought of as Mist Beings. They had no definite form as we think of creatures today, and they were to change in later worlds to living things as we know them.

Although little else existed at that time, the Wóláżhíní Diné'é ("Insect" Beings) had developed a way of life because they recognized the value of making and carrying out plans with the approval of one another.

On the western side of the First World appeared the yellow cloud, and next to it appeared the blue cloud. Where they came together, Áłtsé Asdzáá (First Woman) was formed. With her was a perfect ear of yellow corn. Also with Áłtsé Asdzáá came white shell and turquoise.

The Beings crowded into the female reed and began to climb up inside. The water rose below them and into the giant reed, but the Beings kept ahead of it.

First Man stood on the eastern side of the First World. He represented the Dawn and was the Life Giver. First Woman stood opposite in the West. She represented Darkness and Death.

First Man burned a crystal for fire. The crystal belonged to the male and was the symbol of the mind and of clear seeing. When First Man burned the crystal, it was the mind's awakening. First Woman burned her turquoise for a fire. They saw each other's light and began searching for each other. Three times they were unsuccessful; the fourth time they found each other. First Woman saw that First Man had a crystal for a fire and that it was stronger than her fire. First Man asked her to come and live with him and First Woman agreed.

Many different kinds of Insect Beings lived in the First World. There were *Na'azózii* (Spider Ants), *Tsés'ná* (Wasp People), and *Wóláshiní* (Black Ants). After the Wasps and the different Ant People came *Ni̇́łtságo'* (the Beetles), *Tániil'áii* (the Dragon Flies), *Jaa'abaní* (the Bat People), *Na'ashjé'ii Hastiin* (Spider Man), and *Na'ashjé'ii Asdzą́ą́* (Spider Woman). Many of these different Insects knew the secret of shooting evil and could harm others.

The various Beings disagreed and fought among themselves, and the entire population emerged upward into the Blue World through an opening in the east.

The group moved like clouds, as if on magic carpets, toward the east by gathering some mountain dirt (*Dził łeezh*). With them they took the evils contained in the First World.

Chapter 2

The Second World — The Blue World

Because of the quarreling in the First World, the Beings climbed up to the Blue World. They found many other Beings already living there — *Dólii* (Blue Birds), *Ginítsoh Dootł'izh* (Blue Hawks), *Joo'gii* (Blue Jays), *Táłtł'ááí Ha'ałééh* (Blue Herons), and many other blue-feathered Beings.

There also were larger Insects living in the Second World, like locusts and crickets.

Before leaving the Black World, First Man collected four pillars of light and rolled them into small balls which he carried into the Second World. With the help of Tobacco Horn Worm, who blew smoke at the four balls, they expanded and again became the four pillars of light.

The Second World contained a number of chambers, and First Man and his companions traveled through the various chambers. In one of them lived *Mą'iitsoh* (Wolves), *Náshdółbéi* (Wildcats), *Nahashch'id* (Badgers), *Mą'iiłtsóí* (Kit Foxes) and *Náshdóítsoh* (Mountain Lions). The Wolves lived in a white house in the east. The Wildcats lived in a blue house in the south. The Kit Foxes lived in a yellow house in the west; and the Mountain Lions lived in a black house in the north. The houses were all of different shapes and the Beings living in them were at war with one another.

First Man killed some of the warring animals and then restored them to life because the animals gave him certain songs and prayers as a reward. After that, First Man took off his armor and rested.

Coyote went on his routine, exploring in each of the four directions. Everywhere he went he saw sorrow and suffering. The Beings pleaded to leave. First Man smoked and blew the smoke in the four directions. In this manner he removed the power of evil from the people of the First World which were the Insect Beings. Next, First Man and the others prepared to leave the Second World. First he laid a streak of Zigzag Lightning toward the east; next a streak of Straight Lightning; then

Rainbow, and finally Sun Ray. None of these moved; so he shifted them to the south, to the west and finally to the north. Each time he changed them there was a little reaction, but not enough to allow the people to move into the next world.

First Man then made a *k'eet'áán* (wand) of Jet, Turquoise, Abalone and White Shell. On the wand he placed four footprints so that the Beings could stand on them and be carried up into the next world. The Beings were required to make some *bi yeel* (sacrifice).

Pueblo Pintado in New Mexico   *Nihodeeshgiizh Ch'ínílíní*

Chapter 3

The Third World — The Yellow World

BECAUSE OF THE QUARRELING IN THE SECOND WORLD, the people climbed up to the Yellow World through an opening in the south.

The Bluebird was the first to reach the Third World. After him came the First Four (First Man, First Woman, Coyote and one of the Insects) and then the others.

A great river crossed the land from north to south, and this was the Female River. Also, there was a river flowing from east to west, and this was the Male River. The place where the two rivers crossed is called *Tó Ałnáozlį́* (Crossing of the Waters). It is also called *Tó Bił Dahisk'id* (Place Where the Waters Crossed).

In the Yellow World were six mountains:

        East — *Sis Naajiní* — Dawn, or White Shell Mountain
        South — *Tsoodził* — Blue Bead, or Turquoise Mountain
        West — *Dook'o'oosłííd* — Abalone Shell Mountain
        North — *Dibé Nitsaa* — Obsidian Mountain
        Center — *Dził Ná'oodiłii* — Soft Goods or Banded Rock Mountain
        East of Center — *Ch'ól'į́'į́* — Precious Stones — Gobernador Knob

In the Yellow World there was no sun. *Dootl'iizhii Askii* (Turquoise Boy) lived beyond *Sis Naajiní* to the east. *Yoołgai Asdzą́ą́* (White Shell Woman) lived to the west.

In this world lived *Dlozіłgai* (Squirrels), *Hazéíts'ósii* (Chipmunks), *Na'ats'ǫǫsí* (Mice), *Tązhii* (Turkeys), *Ma'iiłtsóí* (Foxes), *Bįįh* (Deer), *Mósí* (Cat People), *Na'ashjé'ii* (Spider People), *Na'ashǫ́'iiłbáhí* (Lizards) and *Na'ashǫ́'ii* (Snakes). All the people were similar in that they had no definite form.

COYOTE AND BABY WATER MONSTER

First Man had a *dah na'aghízii* (pouch) in which he kept many things. One day, as he was digging into his pouch, a piece of white shell fell out onto the ground. As

Where the Rivers Cross. [Navajo Lake, in northwest New Mexico, covers the spot, the location of which would be somewhere above the little island in the photo.]

Tó Aheedlí

Hosta Butte, near Crownpoint, New Mexico

Ak'i Dah Nást'ání

Gobernador Knob in New Mexico

Ch'óol'į́'į́

The Third World — The Yellow World

the shell hit the ground it flipped. Coyote immediately asked First Man for a small piece. First Man replied that Coyote always asked for things and said things for no reason at all. Coyote kept pleading and First Man gave him a small piece of the white shell.

Coyote took the white shell down to the water's edge where there was a whirlpool. The white shell caused the water to rise and fall. The fourth time the water went down, Coyote saw the child of *Tééhooɫtsódii* (Water Monster). He picked up the baby and hid it under his arms.

Soon afterward, it began to rain, and there came a great flood. When First Man learned from the deer and different birds of the coming of the flood, he sent word to all the Beings and told them to come to *Sis Naajiní* (White Shell Mountain). First Man went to all the six sacred mountains to gather some earth from each one. The water continued to rise, and the people climbed higher and higher on the mountain. First Man planted a cedar tree, hoping to have it reach the top of the sky so that everyone could climb to safety. The tree grew quickly, but it was too short. Next, he planted a pine tree. However, it was not tall enough to reach the top of the sky, either. The third effort by First Man to find a means of escaping the water was to plant a male reed, but it also failed to reach the top of the sky. The fourth attempt was to plant a female reed. It grew to the very top of the sky.

The people crowded into the great female reed and began to climb up. The water followed them as they climbed inside the giant reed. They climbed into the fourth world and came out at a place called *Hajíínéí*. The Turkey was the last animal out of the reed, and the white foam created by the violent water current reached his tail. Today the Turkey still has whitish tail feathers.

As they were entering the Fourth World, the people noticed that Coyote was hiding something. They searched him and found that he was holding Water Monster's baby, *Tééhooɫtsódii Biyázhí*. They reasoned that this had caused the flood. Water Monster was angry because one of his children had been taken by Coyote. (Actually, First Woman was the one who had told Coyote to take the child.) The Beings asked Coyote to take the baby back to the water, which he did. The Water Monster held his head out of the water to receive his baby and to accept an offering. The Beings placed a white shell basket of *Nitł'iz* (precious stones) between his horns. Sure enough, the water began to go down as soon as the child had been returned and the offering placed.

Chapter 4

The Fourth World — The Glittering World

LOCUST'S TESTS

Wíineeshch'įįdii (LOCUST) was the first Being to come into the Fourth World. When he emerged, he was afraid because he saw water everywhere and also many monsters. One of the original inhabitants (monsters) of this world asked Locust from where he had come. Locust answered that he had come from the world beneath this Glittering World. Locust told him that other Beings were coming into this world to live. The monster said that no one could live here unless Locust could pass certain tests. Locust agreed. The first test was to sit in the same place for four days. Locust said he would do that. As the reader knows, a locust has a shell skin which he sheds at certain times; so Locust left his shell skin and made it look as if he were sitting in the same place. While his skin sat there, he burrowed back to the lower world and told the Beings what was happening in the upper world. Locust returned before the four days were up and passed the test.

Next the monster drew an arrow through his body, putting it in his mouth and drawing it out the other end. He challenged Locust to do the same. When Locust equalled the feat, the monster said that he and the rest of the Beings in the lower world could come and live in this world.

SACRED MOUNTAINS

In the Fourth World, First Man and First Woman formed the four main sacred mountains from the soil that First Man had gathered from the mountains in the Third World. When the Beings had assembled the things with which to dress the mountains, they traveled by rainbow to the east to plant the sacred Mountain of the East, *Sis Naajiní*. They put down a blanket of white shell. On top of that they sprinkled some of the soil First Man had brought from the world below, and they

---

Locust — *Wíineeshch'įįdii* — was the first Being
to make his way into the Fourth World.

placed more white shell. This was wrapped up and planted to the east. *Yoołgai Ashkii* (White Bead Boy, or Dawn Boy) was told to enter the Mountain of the East.

Tsoodził (the Mountain of the South) was planted the same way, except that it had a turquoise blanket, soil and pieces of turquoise. *Dootł'izhii At'ééd* (Turquoise Girl) was told to go and live in the Mountain of the South.

Dook'o'oosłíd (the Mountain of the West) was made on an abalone blanket and out of soil and pieces of abalone. *Diichiłí Ashkii* (Abalone Shell Boy) entered the Mountain of the West.

Dibé Nitsaa (the Mountain of the North) was made of an obsidian blanket, soil and pieces of obsidian. *Bááshzhinii At'ééd* (Obsidian Girl) entered the Mountain of the North.

First Man and First Woman fastened the various mountains to the earth. *Sis Naajiní* was fastened with a bolt of white lightning. They covered the mountain with a blanket of daylight and decorated it with black clouds and male rain. The *Shash* (Bear) was sent to guard the doorway of White Bead Boy.

Tsoodził was fastened to the earth with a stone knife. This Mountain of the South was covered with a blue cloud blanket. The mountain was decorated with dark mists and female rain. *Tl'iish Tsoh* (Big Snake) was sent to guard the doorway of Turquoise Girl.

Dook'o'oosłíd was fastened with a sunbeam. This mountain was covered with a yellow cloud. It was decorated with black clouds and male rain. *Niłch'i Diłhił* (Black Wind) was told to guard the doorway for Abalone Boy.

Dibé Nitsaa was fastened to the earth with a rainbow. The mountain was covered with a blanket of darkness, and it was decorated with obsidian. *Atsiniłtl'ish* (lightning) was sent to guard Obsidian Girl's doorway.

FIRE AND SWEAT BATH

The Holy People decided they wanted to make fire and were uncertain about the fire-making procedure. After discussing the matter, they discovered that one of the people had carried flint from the Third World. With it they made the first fire, using the flint on four kinds of wood which were gathered from the four directions. The kinds of wood were fir, piñon, spruce and juniper. The fire made such a noise that it frightened the people. They put another piece of wood on the fire to quiet it, but that did not solve the problem. Finally, one of the people took a branch from another tree and brought it in to calm the fire. The fire quieted down immediately. At that time, the *Honeeshjish* (first poker) was discovered, and the people made a prayer and song for the poker.

The men decided that they wanted to build a sweat bath. The first sweat bath was larger than a hogan. All of the men crowded into the sweat bath, but it would not get warm. Then Lightning came and suggested that they send someone over to a distant place where there was a *Ch'idí* (blanket). A person was sent to bring back the blanket. Owl Man and Owl Woman also had blankets. All of the blankets were used to cover the doorway of the sweat bath, and they helped to get the bath warm. There, in the *Táchééh* (first sweat bath), First Man sang some ceremonial chants and songs. The chants and songs used became sweat bath chants, songs and prayers.

HOGANS

In the sweat bath the men discussed how to build a home. After the bath, when the men returned to where the women were staying, they learned that the women had made a simple forked shelter out of sunflower stalks.

However, *Haashch'éélti'í* (Talking God) showed the people how to make a home out of logs.

The people constructed a hogan of five logs, following Talking God's instructions. The first two logs came from east and west, the next two from south and north, and the fifth from the northeast. In blessing the hogan, they blessed only four sides. Today only four sides of a hogan are blessed. On the roof, where they placed the end of the east log, they put white shell; under the south log, turquoise; under the west log, abalone; under the north log, obsidian, and under the fifth log, jewels from all directions. Where the logs came together at the roof top, they tied feathers of different birds. The tips of the logs are thought to be the eyes of the hogan.

First Man and First Woman told the people that in the future when they built a hogan they must do the same thing and also put pollen underneath and on top. They requested that the hogan be blessed with white and yellow cornmeal, with pollen and with powder from prayer sticks.

After the logs were up and the smaller logs were being added, the people wondered which way the doorway should face. They decided that since all prayers and songs started in the east, they should have the doorway facing east. After deciding upon the doorway, they selected a place where the ashes from the hogan's fire were to be put. Neither charred wood nor bones were to be left inside. This was the first *Ałch'į' adeez'á* (Male hogan) ever built.

The Male hogan was used only for ceremonial gatherings and other religious matters. Food could be brought in when it was time to feed the men engaged in religious activities, but the remains had to be removed as soon as they finished eating. (Some say that the first Male hogan is still in existence, somewhere near the Place of Emergence, and that, at this place, there is still a petrified ladder.)

The Fourth World — The Glittering World

Next they built *Hooghan nímazí* (Female hogan) to the south of the Male hogan. The Female hogan was very different from the Male hogan, both in appearance and function. It was white. It had neither eyes nor the vestibule in the front. In the Female hogan, the children could play and cry, the women could talk and entertain themselves, and the men could tell stories and laugh. Thus, any activities were allowed in the Female hogan, while only religious activities were permitted in the Male hogan.*

MEDICINE AND POISON

After the first sweat bath and the first hogan were completed, the people remembered that something was left down in the Third World. They contacted Water Monster and told him that a valuable medicine had been left behind in the world below. Water Monster plunged into the water to get the medicine and brought it up to the people in the Fourth World. The medicine turned out to be *ánít'įįh* (poison). Everyone asked for some of the medicine, and the people divided it among themselves. *Tł'iish* (Snake) held out his hand and asked for some. When he received his share he placed it in his mouth. Today the snake's bite still is fearful because he placed his share of the medicine in his mouth.

PLANNING AND DEATH

When the first hogan was finished, everyone rested. The first hogan was occupied by First Man and First Woman. Together they planned how things would appear. They discussed that there should be a sun to mark day and night. While the people were planning inside the hogan, a couple of others died outside. No one knew what to do; so they asked Coyote. They told him they were leaving it up to him to decide. Coyote decided that he would take a *Tadzootse'* (Black Rock) and go to *Tódiłhił* (Black Water Lake) to reinforce his decision regarding the dead persons. There he would throw the rock into the lake. If the rock came up and floated, the spirits of the dead persons would go up and there would be no death; if it sank, the spirits would go to the world below and there would be death. When Coyote went to the lake and threw the rock, it sank. That is why the spirits of the dead always go to the world below.

Two days after the persons died, two men looked down the hole through which they had come up into the Fourth World, and they did not see anything and, of course, no tracks. Two days later, they looked again. This time they saw the dead persons sitting in the hole below combing their hair. They went and told the people what they had seen.

---

*This separation of functions of the two kinds of hogans still is observed today.

SUN, MOON AND STARS

The people had the same light as they had had in the worlds below, but they wanted a stronger light to awaken them in the morning; and they wanted a light at night. Also, the people wished to straighten out the night and day and the seasons so that there would be some order in their lives.

They laid stars on a blanket on the ground. *Haashch'ééshzhiní* (Black God) placed the *Sǫ'tsoh* (North Star). First Man placed the *Náhookǫs* (Big Dipper) while First Woman put the *Náhookǫs* (Little Dipper) into the sky. First Man also placed the *Dilyéhé* (Seven Stars) which Black God claimed represented parts of his body. When First Man and First Woman had named the main stars and placed them in the sky, they instructed the stars to guard the sky and man.

Before First Man was finished placing each star in a particular, preselected place in the sky, Coyote came along and asked what they were doing. Coyote picked up a star and put it in the south and said it was his *Sǫ' Doo Nídízídí* (Morning Star). Later, Coyote saw how slowly the naming and placing of the stars was progressing, so he took a corner of the blanket and flipped the remaining stars into the sky. First Man scolded Coyote, but Coyote felt he had done a good job.

After the stars had been placed in the sky, First Man and First Woman still wanted to make something that would give strong daylight. They spread six unwounded buckskins on the ground. On them they placed a large, perfect, round turquoise. They marked the great turquoise with a mouth and nose and eyes. They made a streak of yellow below the mouth, across the face. They then placed another layer of six more unwounded buckskins. This became *Jóhónaa'éí* (the Sun).

The different Beings discussed where they would put the Sun. Some thought it should be placed on the highest mountain, but they finally decided to place it in the sky. The next question was how the Sun should move. Should it move up and down? Should it move in a circle without going down? It was decided that it would pass from east to west to give light all over the world.

Next they placed a perfect white shell on a buckskin. This large, perfect white shell was to become *Tl'éhonaa'éí* (the Moon).

After some difficulty, the Sun and the Moon moved and were placed in the sky. A carrier was selected to carry the Sun and another carrier was selected to carry the Moon.[1] The Sun Carrier and the Moon Carrier declared that every day, as they went on their journey from east to west, someone would die. This would be the price for carrying the Sun and the Moon. Mankind walks the earth at a price and that price is the death of people every day and every night.

1
In some of the stories the Carrier of the Sun was a man on a horse; in other stories the carrier was Turquoise Boy. There is no agreement on this point. The same holds true for the Moon Carrier. In some stories the carrier is a man on a horse; in others, White Shell Girl.

A carrier was selected to carry the Sun.
Another was named to carry the Moon.

Coyote grasped a corner of the blanket
and flipped the remaining stars into the sky.

The Fourth World – The Glittering World

MOCCASIN GAME (SHOE GAME)[2]

There is a place called *Hadahoniiye'bee Hooghan* (the House Made of Banded Rock). The people living there were visited by *Yé'iitsoh Łá'í Naagháii* (One Walking Giant) who spoke and said, "My grandchildren, let us play the moccasin game." The people replied that they did not know how; so he went away.

The next day he returned and again said, "My grandchildren, I would like to play the moccasin game with you."

The people told him, "Grandfather, we do not know the game." Again he left, but he returned on the third day, making the same request, and once again the people said they did not know how.

After he had left for the third time a bird, *Tsé Nináhálééh*, came to the people and said, "The person coming to you is called One Walking Giant. When he comes again asking to play the moccasin game, tell him we will play the game at a place called *Tséłchííyi'* (Red Rock, on the eastern slope of the Lukachukai Mountains) where Big Snake lives. All the Holy People will be there."

One Walking Giant came back the fourth time, saying, "My grandchildren, I have come to play the moccasin game with you."

This time the people replied: "It is well, Grandfather, we will play the game over in *Tséłchííyi'* (Red Rock) where Big Snake lives."

The Giant was very pleased and said, "That is good, my children, that is what I came for." The people said they would send word to the Holy People to gather in four days in Red Rock Canyon to play the Moccasin Game.

All the Holy People assembled together. At the end of the fourth day, One Walking Giant arrived. He had a feather from an eagle which he kept laying against the palm of his hand. From this feather in the Giant's hand, to the moccasin where the *Tólásht'óshí* (little ball) was hidden, there shone a faint ray of light like an almost invisible rainbow. This would help him know in which moccasin the ball was hidden. He had 102 sticks of yucca with him. The number came from the sun's 102 trails.

There are 102 *k'et'ą́ą́z* (yucca counters) in the game. The *tólásht'óshí* (ball) is made from the inside of the yucca plant. The sticks are tied in a bundle and are used as counters to pay the points back and forth. When one side has all 102 points, it wins the game. The people on each side place four moccasins in front of themselves. A small ball is hidden inside one of the four moccasins, and the opposing side guesses where the ball is located. A stick is used to tap the moccasins and to select the exact location of the hidden ball. If the guesser taps once, that means he is guessing the ball is in the moccasin he is tapping. If he taps more than once, that means he is guessing the ball is *not* in the moccasin he is tapping. If the ball happens

---

[2] This story takes place before the destruction of all the Monsters.

to be in the moccasin on which he tapped once, he takes the ball out and gives it to his side.

If he taps more than once on a moccasin, and the ball happens to be in that moccasin, it costs his side 10 counters.

The Giant explained the game to the Holy People and said, "This will not be a free game. All those who travel by day will play against all those who travel by night. The night will bet against the day. The night animals will be on the north side and the day animals on the south. If the night animals win there will be darkness always; if the day animals win there will be light always."

Coyote also came to the canyon to play. He said as long as he howled by both night and day he would be on the winning side, whichever it might be.

The side of darkness used the moccasins of *Shash* (Bear) and *Dahsání* (Porcupine), while the day people's side used the moccasins of *Na'azísí* (Gopher) and *Nahach'id* (Badger).

After explaining the game and its rules, the Giant took a thin piece of corn husk and painted one side black to represent darkness and one side white to represent day. He said he would throw the piece of corn husk into the air. The side of the corn husk which landed upward would tell which team would have the first chance to hide the ball. He let the corn husk fall and the day people called out "gray, gray, gray." The night people called out "black, black, black."

The gray or white side came up; so the day people had the first chance to hide the ball. For a while it looked as if the day people would win, but, finally, a certain night bird hit the moccasin where the ball was hidden and tossed the ball to the night side. Then Owl took the ball and hid it. One time Owl decided not to hide the ball in the moccasin but kept it in his hand. The Giant came over to guess, but he missed, because the ball was not in any of the moccasins. Tears came down his cheeks, and it looked as if the night people might win. As a last resort, the day people sent Gopher under the ground to tunnel up inside each moccasin to discover where the ball was hidden. Gopher reported that the ball was not in any of the four moccasins but rather was hidden in Owl's hand. One of the day birds, armed with this information, went to guess the location of the ball. He pretended to hit each moccasin, but before doing that he said the ball was not there. Finally, he hit Owl's hand and out rolled the ball.

The animals and the Holy People played the game all night but neither side could win all the counters. The animals knew that they must finish the game before daylight and that all night animals must be back in their homes before the sunlight hit them. The night was almost over and neither side had won all the counters. Preparations were made for the animals to return to their homes.

When Owl dropped the ball, all the birds and animals chose whatever designs or colors they wished to wear in the future. *Gáagii* (Crow) and *Shash* (Bear) had fallen asleep. At the last moment the people noticed the approach of dawn. They woke them up hurriedly and told them to get dressed and back to their homes before the

The Fourth World — The Glittering World

dawn came. Crow was in such a hurry that he just dipped himself in the charcoal and became all black. Bear jumped up and reached for his moccasins. Dawn was almost breaking, and he was in such a hurry that he put his moccasins on the wrong feet (his left moccasin on his right foot and vice versa). Today Bear has strangely shaped feet. Then he ran to get into the woods before the sunlight hit him, but he was not quick enough. Just as he was going into the woods the sunlight hit his coat which caused Black Bear to have a reddish sheen to his coat.

Since neither side won, we have both night and day — not all one or the other.

SEASONS

After the people had finished with the Sun and Moon, they began to consider dividing the year into various seasons. First Man and First Woman thought about growing things and animals and when they should plant and harvest. It was decided that the seasons would start with spring when there would be growing things. These growing things would grow, and that would be summer. Then they would get old, and that would be harvest time which would be fall. Then the growing things would be finished and that would be winter. Lightning People were given a time to come, which was in the spring and summer. After winter, they would wake everyone so that all would know that spring had come. It was the responsibility of Lightning People to warn the people, so that they would not tell stories at the wrong time of the year.

HARVEST

First Man brought forth the white corn which he had. First Woman brought the yellow corn. They put the perfect ears of corn side by side. Turkey danced back and forth four times, and out of his feather coat dropped four kernels of corn which were gray, blue, black and red. Next Big Snake came forward, and he gave four seeds which were the pumpkin, the watermelon, the cantaloupe and the muskmelon. The harvest from these seeds was very large.

The Giant explained that those who travel by day would play against those who travel by night — that the night would bet against the day. Here Owl is shown holding the ball in his hand while Gopher burrows up from below and finds that the ball is not in any of the moccasins.

The Fourth World — The Glittering World

THE FIRST ADULTERY

After the harvest, Turquoise Boy visited and slept with First Woman. When First Man returned home he found his wife with Turquoise Boy and was very hurt. This was the first adultery.[3]

At that time there were four leaders: Big Snake, Mountain Lion, Otter and Bear. Usually, every morning First Man would talk to the people, telling them what to do that day. After he found his wife with another man he no longer would come out and talk to the people.

The leaders went to see First Man to find out why he no longer spoke to the people every morning. First Man answered and explained what had happened and why he was worried and deeply concerned. First Man also spoke to his wife, asking her why she had done it. Did she not know that he was responsible for all the good things they enjoyed together? She got angry with her husband, and the conversation led nowhere.

Yellow Fox, Blue Fox and Badger had developed bodily appetites which made them seek out other women, and they further introduced the practice of adultery.

First Man called the leaders and other men together, except those who were responsible for the problem. Together they discussed what should be done. Before a decision was reached, First Man asked for *Nádleeh* (the hermaphrodite) to come to him. He asked whether *Nádleeh* could cook and prepare food, weave and fix men's hair. He asked whether *Nádleeh* had the proper utensils to carry out those tasks. *Nádleeh* replied that he knew how to do these things, which usually were performed by women, and that he had the proper utensils.

THE SEPARATION

The leaders and First Man decided to separate themselves (the males) from the women. They decided to build a *Naashkǫǫ'* (raft) and take all the men over to the other side of the river. The place the men crossed was where water flowed together,

---
[3]
The identity of the offending parties varies from story to story. In one, for example, the husband was Wolf and his wife was seduced by Handsome Yellow Fox.

The men decided to prove that the women could not get along without them.

The Fourth World — The Glittering World

and there was a rushing of water, which made it almost impossible to cross. With great difficulty, the men reached the other side. They wanted to prove that the women could not get along without them. The leaders decided to leave the four guilty men (Yellow Fox, Blue Fox, Badger and Turquoise Boy) with the women. It was thought that, since these men wanted the women so badly, they would be left behind.

When the men left, the women laughed and made merry. They said that the women did not need them and were happy to be rid of them. Besides, they had several handsome men still with them. At first the women did not mind being alone. They planted a small field just as the men planted a corn field on their side of the river.

The men who were left with the women soon became exhausted from trying to meet the sexual demands of so many women. Their desires, which had been so strong earlier, quickly disappeared. Later the men lost their voices, and even their noses became smaller as a result of the physical demands of the women.

On the other side of the river, *Nádleeh* ground the corn and cooked the food so that the men did not suffer. In a few years, however, the women became lazy. They did not take care of their small field, and it grew only weeds. At times, some of the women attempted to cross the river to rejoin the men, but the swift and strong current carried them off, and they were drowned. The women used strange objects to satisfy their lustful passions. The result was the birth, later, of giants and monsters. Some of the men also attempted to satisfy their desires through the use of the liver of a recently-killed deer. Those who took part in this practice were struck by lightning. On the other side of the river the women were very hungry, and their clothes were ragged. They called the men to show how thin they were, and they asked to be taken back.

The leaders held a council. All felt that, if women disappeared, it would be bad. As a result, the leaders decided to take the women back. Cleansing ceremonies were held to purify both the men and the women. After the proper ritual and sweat baths, both sexes were purified and returned to live with each other.

MONSTERS

First Man and First Woman lived near *Dził Ná'oodiłii* (Huerfano Mountain). These two were the first Beings to appear like the people we now know as humans. The living things that came from the worlds below were similar to spirits; they were the Holy People.

The population began to increase, and the crops were good; but there were monsters who killed people and caused great concern. As mentioned above, they were the result of the actions of the women in the lower world during the Separation of the Sexes. The people were very afraid of the monsters.

The Fourth World — The Glittering World

At this time people were living at Pueblo Bonito, and these, like the early Navajos, were threatened by the monsters. *Yé'iitsoh* (Big Monster) lived on top of Mount Taylor. He would hit the people with his clubs of black, blue, yellow and varicolored flint. He used them for food.

Déélgééd (Horned Monster) roamed over the land. He had very keen eyesight and was similar to a rhinoceros. He lived in the valley where wild cotton grew. If someone passed near him, he would chase and kill the person with his horns or simply run over him.

The *Tsé Nináhálééh* (Bird Monsters) lived on the pinnacles of *Tsé Bit'a'í* (Shiprock). There were a mother, a father and two youngsters. The parents would fly and pick up people for food and drop them into the nest. The fall would kill the people. Then the youngsters would eat them.

Tsédahódzííłtáłii (Monster That Kicked People Off the Cliff) sat leaning back against Kicking Rock. As people walked by, he kicked them off the trail and over the edge of the cliff. Down below, the monster's children devoured the victims.

Bináá'yee'agháanii (Monster That Killed With His Eyes) stared at his captives until they were hypnotized. He then ate them.

There were many more monsters, too — *Tsé' Ahéénídiłii* (Crushing Rock), *Séít'áád* (Moving Sand), *Jadí Naakits'áadah Náhiníléí* (Twelve Antelopes), *Shash Na'ałkaahii* (Tracking Bear) and others.

While all this was happening, First Man and First Woman were living at the foot of *Dził Ná'oodiłii*, "Mountain Around Which Moving Was Done." They had been told that when the people had multiplied, Changing Woman would be born.

ASDZĄ́Ą́ NÁDLEEHÉ (CHANGING WOMAN)

One morning at dawn, First Man and First Woman saw a dark cloud over *Ch'óol'į́'į́* (Gobernador Knob). Later they heard a baby cry. When they looked to see where the crying was coming from, they realized that it came from within the cloud that covered the top of *Ch'óol'į́'į́*. First Man searched and found a baby girl. She was born of darkness and the dawn was her father.

Huerfano Mountain in New Mexico

Dził Ná'oodiłii

The Fourth World — The Glittering World

First Man and First Woman brought her up under the direction of the Holy People. They fed her on sun-ray pollen, pollen from the clouds, pollen from the plants and the dew of flowers. This baby became *Asdzą́ą́ Nádleehé* (Changing Woman), one of the most loved of Navajo Holy People.

When she became of age (reached puberty), a ceremony was held over her called *Kinaaldá* (Walked Into Beauty). This same ceremony is given today for Navajo girls when they reach puberty, except that Changing Woman lay on a pile of blankets facing west, whereas today the girl must face the east. Changing Woman said the girl must face the east so that she can look at earth and sky.

The first *Kinaaldá* was performed by the Holy People who were living on the earth at the time. They wanted to hold this ceremony for Changing Woman so that she would be able to have children. It was held at *Ch'óol'į́'į́* (Gobernador Knob).

First Woman gave instructions to Changing Woman regarding what she must do in the *Kinaaldá* ceremony. First Woman said, "You must run four times in the direction of the rising sun. As you turn to come back, you must make the turn sunwise."

Pueblo Bonito, Chaco Canyon in New Mexico
Tsé Bíyah Anii'áhí

Shiprock in New Mexico   *Tsé Bit'a'í*

When Changing Woman (White Shell Woman) came of age (reached puberty) a ceremony was held over her called "Walked into Beauty." This same *Kinaaldá* is performed today for Navajo girls when they reach puberty.

The Fourth World — The Glittering World

When First Woman decorated Changing Woman, she said, "Sit down here, my daughter." Then she spread out an unwounded buckskin. On it she placed a piece of turquoise, one of abalone, one of obsidian and a white bead. Then she put white bead moccasins on the girl's feet. She gave her leggings and a skirt of white beads. She designed her sleeve fringes with white beads and made her wristlets of white beads. Then First Woman decorated her neck with white beads, turquoise beads, abalone shell beads and obsidian beads. She gave earrings to Changing Woman, and she placed her hand on the girl's forehead and moved the hand over the length of Changing Woman's head. In this way everything was to grow in the future. Finally, she placed a white bead head plume in the girl's hair.

To the east the bluebird gave its call; from the south the dark small bird called; in the west the wild canary gave its call, and from the north came the call of the corn beetle. First Man and First Woman were pleased. The calls announced the coming of the Holy People for the fourth night of the ceremony.

First Man said, "This is Changing Woman who now is to be called White Bead Woman because she has dressed herself in white beads." Some of the Holy People objected to this and said they would continue to call her Changing Woman. A large cake was baked for the Sun, and this was given to him the next morning.

Talking God was asked to make some songs for the ceremony, and he replied, "My mouth is not used to it; so I will sing only four Hogan Songs."

Áłtsé Hashké (First Scolder) said, "What do you mean, just four Hogan Songs? Don't be foolish. You must sing more than four. Your tail feathers number twelve and you should therefore sing twelve Hogan Songs."

Talking God agreed and answered, "So be it." Then he placed a rainbow across the hogan from east to west and another rainbow from south to north. He made the hogan larger by blowing on each side, beginning with the east. On the east side Talking God planted a row of 12 white beads in the shape of tail feathers; on the south he planted 12 turquoise beads in the shape of tail feathers; on the west side he planted 12 tail-feather-shaped abalone shell beads, and on the north he planted a row of 12 tail-feather-shaped jet beads.

When this was done, all those present were very happy. Talking God sang his 12 Hogan Songs, and the others gave their own set of songs.

As time passed, Changing Woman felt lonely and wandered away from her hogan. She sat in the sun by a small waterfall. There she lay down and slept. When she awoke she felt tired, and she was sure someone had just slipped away from sleeping beside her. She saw tracks which had come from the east, and she saw where the tracks had left.

In time, she had twins. Both were boys. As the boys grew up, their mother adored them and gave them much love. When they still were small, they had their first bows and arrows. They would go hunting for small game and bring back rabbits and squirrels. The boys exercised daily, wrestling and running. They would race to the east to the top of a mountain in the morning. There they would breathe in the sunlight as it came out from behind the mountains to the east. When it snowed, they would roll in the snow, stripped of their clothing. Soon they were very strong.

As the boys grew older, they asked their mother who their father was. Their mother did not answer.

She always cautioned the boys not to go too far from the hogan because the monsters might catch them. Changing Woman was worried all the time. She was afraid the monsters might catch her boys and eat them. One day the boys were playing close to their home. Suddenly the earth shook, warning them that a monster was getting close. The boys quickly ran home to hide. The monster walked up to their hogan and demanded that the two boys, whose tracks he saw leading to the hogan, come out. Changing Woman told the monster that no one else lived in the hogan. The monster mentioned the tracks which led into the hogan. Changing Woman said that she had made the tracks herself. She said she was so lonely that often she would go outside and make children's tracks in the sand, using her hands just to make believe that there were children around. This satisfied the monster and he left.

THE TWINS GO TO THEIR FATHER

One of the Twins, later to be known as *Naayéé' Neezghání* (Monster Slayer), was the older, braver and more daring. His brother, *Tó Bájísh Chíní* (Child Born of Water), was younger and not as strong. Both boys had dreams and visions.

One day as the Twins were out on one of their many hunting trips, they discovered a tiny hole in the ground with smoke drifting out of it. This happened *álílee* (through a miraculous power). They stopped and looked at the hole with curiosity. One of them touched it, and a voice called from within, "Come in." With that, the hole widened enough so that the boys could crawl in. The sunlight revealed a ladder going into the hole, and they climbed down. When they reached the bottom, they came face to face with *Na'ashjé'ii Asdzáá* (Spider Woman). They were astounded, as they looked around, by the beautifully decorated walls, covered with feathers of every description and color. Collecting feathers of all existing birds was Spider Woman's hobby.

Spider Woman asked them, "What are you doing here, my children?" One of the boys responded that they were on a hunting trip. At that time, the Sun was about midway between noon and sundown.

One of the boys again spoke up, saying, "We and our people are being troubled by monsters. We want to know who our father is so that we can ask him to help us destroy the monsters." To this, Spider Woman answered, "I know all about it. I know who your father is."

At that very moment the Sun stopped, and his rays quivered. The Sun remained fixed in the sky while Spider Woman was telling the boys all she knew about their father, *Jóhónaa'éí* (the Sun). When she finished, she said she would help

Changing Woman had twins, both of whom were boys.

The Fourth World — The Glittering World

the Twins to see their father so that they could get his help to kill the *naayéé'* (monsters).

She warned the boys of the obstacles they would have to overcome to reach their destination. To help them, Spider Woman taught them things that only she knew.

During their stay at Spider Woman's place, the boys were shown her great wealth. First she opened a door to the east, then to the south, to the west and finally to the north. In every direction were things of great value — like precious stones and things that are essential to the *Diné* of today.

Spider Woman was very kind to them. She said, "I do not have much to eat, but I will share what I have." She took out meal and seeds and put them in four baskets which she placed in front of the boys. In the first basket she put white corn meal, in the second and third three kinds of seeds and in the fourth basket she placed beeweed meal. She put only a little in each basket, and the Twins thought it was not enough, but they said nothing. She knew what they were thinking and said, "There is plenty." As the boys ate, the baskets kept filling, and they were not able to finish the food. When they had eaten all they could hold, the boys rubbed themselves on their legs and bodies.[4]

---

[4] A sign of appreciation.

Father of the Twins — the Sun *Jóhónaa'éí Hataa'lá*

The Fourth World — The Glittering World

While the older brother was eating, Spider Woman dropped a small piece of turquoise into his corn meal. She dropped a piece of white shell into the corn meal of the younger twin. She also gave a *Hiinááh bits'os* (magic eagle feather) to each boy and told them the feathers would help them when they were in trouble. The piece of turquoise and piece of white shell they had swallowed were to make their hearts strong and to give them courage.

The Twins stayed there to learn what the Spider Woman knew about the journey they were to undertake.

"About your journey, it won't take a day; it will take a long time," she said. Their trip was going to be so hazardous and difficult that they had to learn, by heart, the chants and the prayers that were to keep them from harm.

In order to pass the frightful guardians that they would meet on their way to the Sun's house, the boys had to call each by a certain name, then utter a prayer. All this they learned during their stay with Spider Woman. She told them that after leaving her home, their first obstacle would be *Lók'áá' Adigishii* (Reeds That Cut). These reeds were so sharp that they would cut, even though they just barely and lightly touched a person. From this cut the individual would bleed to death. That was why it was necessary to say the prayers and to call the reeds by their special name before attempting to pass them. Spider Woman also warned the boys that, by the time they reached the watering place near the reeds, they would be so thirsty that they would want to ignore the dangers that existed at this particular place. It was the promise of cool, clear water that lured many victims to their bloody deaths caused by the sharp reeds.

Spider Woman said that the next hazard would be *Séít'áád* (Moving Sand). There was no way around it. When a person tried to climb up, the sand would slide the person down to the bottom again. As the person fell, the sand would cover him. The boys could cross the Moving Sand only by uttering the right prayer and chant and by calling it by its given name.

Next they had to pass through the *Tsé' Ahéenínídił* (Canyon Which Closed in on a Traveler). The Twins were told that if they could not stop the canyon from crushing them, even after they had called its name and uttered prayers and chants, they were to use the magic feathers which Spider Woman had given them especially for that purpose. She also told them that there would be a messenger behind them who would whisper in their ears, telling them what to do after they had passed through the canyon.

Following passage through this treacherous canyon, they were to continue on their journey until they reached the *Tsé Yót'ááhí'aii* (Four Pillars of Rocks) that represented old age. Spider Woman warned them not to pass on the shady side, because, if they did so, they would die of old age. Instead, she told them to pass on the sunny side (the south side).

Beyond the massive pillars, they had to cross the *Nahodits'ǫ'* (Wash That Swallowed), and they were to do certain things to avoid getting killed — saying the

38

prayers and the chants and calling the wash by its right name. To cross the wash, they also would have to ride the *Wóóshiyishí* (Measuring Worm).

When the boys finally reached the ocean, they were supposed to ride the rest of the way to the Sun's home on a *Tátłkáá' Dijádii* (Water Skeeter). They would have to explain to the insect why they wanted the ride, and they would have to say a few prayers and chants before they could get the ride.

Spider Woman explained that upon reaching the Sun's home, the Twins would encounter four obstacles who served as doormen to the Sun's home. First there was *Tł'iish tsoh Dooniniti'ii* (Gigantic Snake), then *Shashtsoh* (Huge Black Bear), then *Ii'ni'bikạ'ịị* (Big Thunder), and, finally, *Níyoltsoh* (Big Wind). There were prayers and chants that they learned properly to get past these guardians.

It took quite a while for the Twins to get all this information from Spider Woman. Finally, they were ready to start on their journey. They set out, carrying the magic feathers and being followed by the messenger. After traveling for a long time, they came to the place of *Lók'áá' Adigishii* (Reeds That Cut). The place looked just as Spider Woman had described it, with cool water coming out of a spring. They could see bones everywhere, and they knew these were the bones of victims who had not known danger existed there or who had not known how to avoid the danger. The Twins realized that this was the first hazard; so they said the prayer, sang the chants and called the reeds by the right name. (The names the boys called these dangerous obstacles are known to the people who are acquainted with the complete story. The names are very powerful.) The reeds were so happy to hear their right name and to hear the prayers and chants that plumes sprang out from the tops of their stalks. The two boys drank the cool water without any danger from the reeds. They drank their fill and left without being bothered by the cutting reeds.

The Twins then traveled for a long time, until they got to *Séít'ááḍ* (Moving Sand). They prayed and chanted, called it by name and started climbing up. As they climbed higher through the sand, they encountered piles of bones. Shuddering, the twins passed without being injured.

Next, they came to the canyon which Spider Woman had told them they had to pass through. As they started into it, the walls began to close upon them. They called the canyon by name, but the walls kept on coming together. The boys were so afraid that neither was able to utter the proper prayers and chants. Just before the walls closed in completely, they stepped onto their magic feathers and floated to safety, with the canyon crashing shut just beneath their feet. The boys were badly shaken by this close call, but they continued on.

Before long they reached the four old, graying *Tsé Yót'ááhí'áii* (Four Pillars of Rocks), each one grayer than the one before. They must have forgotten what Spider Woman had told them, or perhaps they preferred the broad, shady trail on the north to the narrow sunny one on the south side. They disregarded the warnings given them and started along the trail on the north side. As they passed the first pillar of rock, they saw that some of their hairs became tipped with white; after the next

Spider Woman warned them that, after leaving her home, their first obstacle would be *Lók'áá' Adigishii* (Reeds That Cut).

They called the canyon by name, but the walls continued to close. So afraid were the boys that neither was able to say the proper prayers and chants. However, just before the walls closed in completely, the Twins stepped on their magic feathers and were floated rapidly to safety, with the canyon crashing shut just beneath their feet.

one, there were streaks which were very noticeable. At that moment, the protective messenger who had been following them sent some birds to change their course. Then the messenger told them the right way to go; so they changed their route and passed the last pillars on the sunny side, even though the trail was very narrow and sheer. The trail was so steep that the Twins did not dare look down for fear that they might get dizzy and fall. They realized, with great fear, that, had they passed on the shady side of the fourth pillar, they would have died of old age.

They continued on their journey to the "Wash That Swallowed." There they met *Wóóshiyishí* (Measuring Worm). They talked to him and explained their needs. The worm agreed to take them across. *Wóóshiyishí* said, "Hang on tight, for I'm going to snap (or spring) across." The boys were now past middle age because of their mistake back at the four pillars. They got on the back of this creature and held tightly. Just as he had said he would do, the worm sprang right across.

The Twins continued on their journey to the Sun. After a long period of time, they finally came to the shore of the ocean and asked one of the *Tátkáá' Dijádii* (Water Skeeters) to take them across. Beyond the place known as "Darkness," they rode the *Tátkáá' Dijádii* all the way to the home of the Sun. There they saw the four guardians about whom they had been told. The Twins passed them safely with the aid of the prayers, the chants and the knowledge of the names of the guardians.

They went through a great doorway and saw a woman sitting there. She said sternly, "What are you doing here? This is no place for land people. Who are you?"

They answered, "We have come to see our father, the Sun." The Twins could see that the woman was surprised.

"What are you talking about?" she said. The Sun had told her that he left every morning with but one thing in mind — to do what had been selected as his task, which was to carry the Sun disk.

"What do you mean, he is your father?" she asked.

After the Sun's wife got over her anger, the Twins told her how they had found out who their father was. Then they looked for the room in which the Sun stayed after his return from his daily journey. As they walked into the room, they repeated some prayers and chants. All this time the Sun's wife had been trying to get the Twins to leave, for she feared for their safety when the Sun returned. However, they had seen their lives threatened too many times to become afraid now.

In the evening the Sun returned and asked, "Where are the people I saw entering my house?"

The Sun's wife said, "There are no people here. I don't know what you are talking about." She was afraid the Sun would try to kill the two boys when he found them. The older twin was wrapped in a *nohodeetł'iish* (blue cloud) and placed over the doorway to the east, while the younger twin was wrapped in a *k'os dithił* (black cloud) and placed on the south side. Each boy had his magic feather next to his heart.

The Fourth World — The Glittering World

Finally, the Sun's wife told him that two boys had come asking for their father. She scolded him for saying he never bothered any other women, when evidently he had at least two children by some other woman.

The Sun searched the house and finally found the Twins. The Twins explained why they had undertaken the long and dangerous journey to visit the Sun, their father. At the end of the explanation, the Sun said nothing. He did not think the boys were his sons; so he decided to test them to find out.

The Sun prepared tobacco and asked the Twins to smoke. The tobacco was very strong and would kill persons unless they were protected, as the Twins were. They smoked four times, and, after each smoke, the boys said they felt fine.

After the smoking test, the Sun prepared a sweat bath for the Twins. Inside, at the rear of the sweat bath, the daughter of the Sun dug a separate pit and covered it with sheets of white shell and Darkness. She also put Evening Twilight, Sky Blue and Dawn as curtains over the doorway. The daughter told the boys to hide in this pit in

Canyon Which Closed on a Traveler Tsé' Ahéenínídił

Wash That Swallowed Nahodits'o'

The Sun's daughter explained to the Twins how to hide in the pit in the back of the sweat bath so that they would be protected from the heat. The Sun tried to make the heat so great that it would destroy the Twins, but, each time he asked how they felt, they told him they were fine.

The Sun did not want to give the weapon to the Twins because it was so powerful and because they would use it to kill the monsters, some of whom were his children, just as were the Twins. Finally, however, he agreed to allow them to use the weapon.

The Fourth World — The Glittering World

the back of the sweat bath to protect themselves from the heat. The Sun tried to make the heat so great that it would destroy the Twins, but, each time he asked how they were doing in the sweat bath, they told him they were just fine. At that point, the Sun began to believe that the boys must be his sons, since no human being could live in that intense heat.

Still the Sun subjected the Twins to additional tests. He gave them corn meal that was poisoned. Then the Sun threw them against big, sharp, many-colored *béésh doolghasii* (flint knives). But again they were not harmed. This time their magic feathers protected them.

Finally, the Sun recognized that the Twins were truly his sons, and he had his daughter bathe them. The Twins were washed first in a white bead basket, next in a turquoise basket, then in a white shell basket and last in a black obsidian basket. Next, the Sun molded and shaped the Twins' arms, legs, fingers, faces and bodies. He dressed them in beautiful clothes, and they were very handsome.

The Sun then took the Twins and showed them around his house, telling them to choose anything they wanted for themselves. They looked in four different rooms: In the east room were fields of the finest corn and other plants and seeds; in the south room were wild animals of all kinds and descriptions; in the west room were domesticated animals including horses, and in the north room were precious jewels of all kinds. The Twins explained they would need all these things later, but that they were not what they had come for on this trip.

The Twins again explained that the earth people were being destroyed by the monsters and they needed means to destroy those monsters. On the wall of the Sun's house, above the north door, hung a weapon. The Twins asked for that weapon It looked like a bow and arrow but it really was lightning. The Sun asked them what they would do with the weapon, and they said they would use it to kill the monsters. The Sun was reluctant to give it to the Twins because it was so powerful and because they would use it to kill the monsters. Some of the monsters were his children, just as the Twins were. Finally he agreed to give them the lightning.

The Twins also were given suits of flint armor. The older boy was dressed in dark flint and the younger in blue flint. The Sun said the older boy would be named Monster Slayer and the younger would be called Child Born of Water.

He handed the older brother his weapon, *Atsiniltł'ish k'aa'* (Lightning That Strikes Crooked). He handed the younger brother his weapon which also was lightning, *Hatsoo'algha k'aa'* (Lightning That Flashes Straight).

The Sun promised to help the Twins kill the monsters. He told them that *Yé'iitsoh* had four lightning arrows and that they must get all of them. The Sun asked for a tail feather from the headdress of *Yé'iitsoh* as a reward for helping the boys.

Monster Slayer and Child Born of Water then returned to the earth. The Sun had told them that when killing the monsters the older must do the killing and the younger must watch his firebrand which would show how the older brother was progressing.

Chapter 5

Asdzą́ą́ Nádleehé [Changing Woman]

To indicate the close similarities, with only minor differences, in Navajo stories, the following version of Changing Woman and the Twins' journey to their father is presented. This version was told by the late "Chic" Sandoval, a Navajo who lived near Lukachukai and who knew many Navajo stories. The story is included in just the manner it was told by Mr. Sandoval in 1968.

• • • • • • • • • • • •

WHEN THE PEOPLE CAME UP from the world below, or after they moved to the place we call *Dził Ná'ooditii* (Banded Rock Mountain), they lived there for some time until, eventually, they began to split up. First Man and First Woman were aware of the problems that the people were discussing and what they were planning to do; so each time some problem came up, they would tell Coyote to go and investigate.

"See what is going on over there. People are meeting to discuss a certain issue. Go over and correct them." That's why Coyote always was butting in on someone else's business, but it was done on the instruction of First Man and First Woman.

Time went on, but we had no way of telling time. One morning, as any other morning, First Man got up early and took a walk before the Sun was up. He noticed a mountain, the one called *Ch'óol'į́'į́* (Gobernador Knob), capped with fog. That began to worry him. He wondered: "What is that fog on top of the mountain?"

The mountain was shaped like an ant hill, and the tip of it was hidden by the fog.

He decided to go there to investigate. He came to the mountain and he circled it and came up from the east. Then First Man went back down Gobernador Knob and came back up from the south. Again he just took a quick look before going back down. He did the same thing from the west and from the north, each time descending. Finally, he returned to the east and went all the way to the top. On the sand was lying a new-born baby girl. He didn't believe it. "Imagination," he thought;

47

Unbelieving, First Man, to be sure that a baby really was on the mountain, climbed to the top from the east, south, west and north. Then he repeated the procedure. Finally, going up from the east again, he approached the baby girl who was lying on the sand.

Asdzą́ą́ Nádleehé (Changing Woman)

so he went back down and came up from the south side and looked again. Still, there was the baby. Again he went back down and came up from the west side. The baby still was there. To make sure, he walked around to the north. From there he looked down, and the baby was still there. Now he was certain that a baby was really lying there in the sand, so he retraced his steps and came up from the east side of the mountain. He looked at the baby. (Nobody knows the mother or the father of the baby.)

Just then Talking God came running over and claimed the baby. First Man asked him, "How do you expect to raise her?"

"I can use pollen," replied Talking God.

"Feed her pollen? Pollen isn't food. You cannot raise a child on pollen," answered First Man.

Talking God asked, "Then, what are you going to feed this child?"

"Well, I go hunting. I hunt for rabbits, deer and other game. When I bring in the meat, I will cook it and feed her the broth. That is how I will raise her," said First Man. He finally persuaded Talking God to let him, First Man, care for the baby. So, home went First Man, taking the baby to First Woman. Together, they would raise her.

At about that same time Salt Woman came into the family. With her help First Man and First Woman were able to raise the little girl. Coyote always was nearby, too. During the same period, the threat of the monsters was becoming serious. They were roaming around, picking up people and carrying them away.

Some say it took the child only four days to grow up. Still, some say it was four years. Whichever way it happened, nobody knows. She grew up to be a beautiful young lady. She became known as White Shell Woman, and later, Changing Woman, the mother of the Navajo clans. When she arrived at adulthood, a puberty ceremony was performed for her. Talking God appeared as the main singer, and invitations were extended to many other Holy People. They all attended and sang their songs. This is still practiced today. There usually is one person who conducts the proceedings, and he usually starts the singing. After he goes through his songs, anyone who wants to sing can do so. All this started the time this particular ceremony, *Kinaaldá*, was performed for Changing Woman. Two such ceremonies were performed for her before she was ready for marriage. Then she had become a woman.

One day Changing Woman was out gathering wood, just before sundown. She had the wood all tied. As she tried to pick up the wood to take home, some irresistible force held it down, and she could not stand up. She looked around but

Asdzą́ą́ Nádleehé (Changing Woman)

no one was nearby. Every time she tried to lift up the bundle of wood, something held it down. After the fourth attempt, she looked up and saw a young handsome man standing near her. He was the Sun.

She visited with him, and, after that, she went down to a spring to get some water. The story goes that every time she went there, she would lie down under that dripping water to enjoy the pleasure that it gave her. From her relations with the Sun, she gave birth to two boys. Some say they were twins and others say they were not — that one was born, and, after some time, the other was born. Some say they were twins born almost at the same time.

The first of the twins, or boys, later was to be called Monster Slayer. He was the one who would get rid of the monsters so that the human race could increase in number. The second later was to be called Child of Water because he was born for the water which was dripping at the waterfall.

After the two boys were born, it was very dangerous because of the roaming giants, who would pick people up and carry them away. All around Huerfano Mountain there were planted many cacti. That is why, to this day, there are a lot of cacti at that location. The cacti were planted to keep the giants away. These giants did not wear any clothing or shoes, so, naturally, they could not walk in the cacti.

The boys grew up together, and their grandfather, First Man, made ordinary bows and arrows for them to use. They got to playing around one day and saw a buzzard fly by. They took aim and shot him. This made the buzzard angry; so he prepared his own arrows and a bow out of his wing feather. The buzzard said to himself, "I can shoot, too." He is the head of the witches and uses the "bean shooter." The boys were supernaturally protected so that the beans did not have any effect.

As they grew up, every night they would ask their mother, "Who is our father?"

She would not tell them. "I cannot tell you," she repeated. "You have a father, but he is dangerous. He might kill you."

But they kept asking, "Who is our father? Where does he live? Where is he?" But their mother would not tell them.

Each night, when the boys retired, the two women, Salt Woman and Changing Woman, would sit and talk across from where the boys were. The boys would listen. They soon became curious. They wanted to know what the two ladies talked about.

They kept insisting that their mother tell them who their father was. Finally, someway or another, they became aware that their father was the Sun, who lived in the east.

The boys wanted to go there and see their father. All of a sudden they had a notion to take off toward the east to find the Sun. They started without telling their mother or anybody else where they were going. They just took off. As they were going along on a flat place, they saw smoke coming out of the earth. They stopped and looked down into the hole where the smoke was coming from. There they saw an old lady sitting. The lady said, "Come on down, my grandchildren."

Changing Woman, also known as White Shell Woman and White Bead Woman, would lie down under the dripping water for the pleasure that it gave her.

Asdzą́ą́ Nádleehé (Changing Woman)

"What for?" asked the boys.

The lady repeated, "Just come on down here"; so they climbed down to where the old lady was sitting. This lady happened to be Spider Woman. There were webs all over the ceiling and the walls of her home. She is the one who presented them with plumes, which were shields that would protect them on their journey.

She said, "My grandchildren, you shall take these along for your protection. There are many dangerous places between here and where you are going. Every time you meet these obstacles, use the feathers to protect yourselves."

After leaving Spider Woman's home, they came to a place where there was a big sand hill that you couldn't climb over. Every time you started going up, you would slide back to where you started from. The boys used the feathers to pass this sand dune, and they continued their journey.

Soon they came to a place where there were a lot of reeds which were as sharp as knives. When the wind blew, it was impossible to go through. As soon as you stepped in there, the reeds would cut you to pieces.

Before they started through the reeds, Black God, the Fire God, approached them. He asked, "My grandchildren, where are you headed?" The boys told him that they were going to see their father. "He's a dangerous man," said Black God.

"We can't cross these cutting reeds," said the boys.

Black God answered, "I can take care of that." He set the reeds afire and soon the boys were able to pass through the reeds and continue their journey.

At another place, they came to a narrow canyon. Every time they tried to step across, the canyon would open up and smash together. If a victim stepped into the canyon, the canyon would come together and crush him. The boys stood at the edge of this canyon, not knowing how to cross. Suddenly, they saw a worm who asked, "Where are you going, my grandchildren?"

"We are going to see our father," answered the boys.

The worm warned, "He is a strong man. You had better be careful."

"We cannot cross this canyon," said the boys.

"I can cross it," said the worm. "Get on my back and I will take you both across."

The worm bridged the canyon with his body, and the boys crossed.

Before they came to the ocean, they encountered more of the dangerous obstacles which they successfully passed with the help of the feathers. When they finally came to the ocean in the east, there was no way for them to cross. Their father's home was floating far out on the ocean. Again they received help, and the boys arrived at their father's house.

When they reached the Sun's home, there was a beautiful young lady sitting there. This was the Sun's wife. She said, "Strangers, who are you? What are you doing here?"

They told her of their journey and why they had come. She shook her head and said, "Your father is a dangerous man. He will surely kill you both. He returns

Asdzáá Nádleehé (Changing Woman)

home after he goes down in the west." Then she picked up the roll of curtain (cloud) she had on the east side of the hogan. It was white. She wrapped them up in it and replaced it on the wall. There was a blue curtain (cloud) on the south side, a yellow one on the west and a black one on the north.

A little after sunset, the earth began to tremble and roar. The Sun was coming. He walked in and said, "I saw someone coming in here at noon. Who was it?"

The Sun's wife would not say anything because she was jealous that he had fathered children elsewhere. This is where all jealousy got started. The Sun kept after her, and finally she said, "Yes, there is somebody here waiting for you. Here you have been telling me you are innocent and that you were faithful to me. You have not been faithful to me. Some of your children are here looking for you."

He said, "Where are they?" He received no answer; so he grabbed the dark curtain on the north and unravelled it and found nothing. He repeated this until he got to the curtain on the east side where the boys were hiding.

As the Sun unravelled the curtain, the boys fell out hard, but because of the sacred feathers, they did not suffer any injuries.

He asked, "What do you want? What are you after? Where are you from?" The boys told the Sun why they had come. Still the Sun did not believe and trust the boys. The Sun picked up the boys and threw them at sharp spikes that hung in the east. The boys bounced off unharmed. Then he tried it again to the south and then to the west and finally to the north. Still, the boys were uninjured. Next, he ordered one of his servants to take the boys out and lay them in the ocean so they would freeze to death. But the beaver came along and covered the boys with her hide to keep them warm all night.

The next morning at dawn, they were brought back to the Sun's home. The Sun's attempt to freeze the boys had failed. Next, the Sun ordered another of his servants to prepare a sweat house and give the boys a sweat bath. He wanted to suffocate them.

The servant went and prepared the sweat house, but he dug a secret chamber into the side like a gopher. Then he placed four stones, one after another over the hole to block the heat. Afterward, the boys went into the sweat house, having been told of the secret hole into which they could go for protection from the extreme heat. This they did. As they climbed into the secret chamber, the four stones were placed on top to protect the boys from the heat. Soon the stones were red hot. After a certain amount of time, the Sun came to the doorway and said, "Are you hot?"

The boys said, "No." The Sun asked that question four times. After the fourth time, he poured water on the stones to create steam in the sweat bath. But the rocks protected the boys from the scalding steam.

The room was filled with steam when the Sun asked again, "Are you hot now?"

"Yes," said the boys.

Spider Woman instructed the Twins, "Every time you meet these obstacles, use the feathers to protect yourselves."

"Come out, now," said the Sun. The boys came out, unharmed by the heat and the steam.

Next, the Sun tried the boys with another test. This test was poisoned tobacco that he had prepared. The boys were warned, supernaturally, of the poisoned tobacco the Sun was offering them and that they should not inhale the smoke. The boys did not inhale the smoke and slipped some kind of an antidote into the tobacco to make it ineffective. Thus the boys were able to get through another test.

Finally, the Sun admitted that the boys were his children. He called his daughter, who was the child of the woman the boys found in the Sun's home when they arrived. The daughter was very beautiful; and there also was a son, who was as good looking as the girl. The daughter used her brother to mold the two boys in the likeness of his features. This molding was carried on by The People for some time, but I do not know whether it still is practiced for males.

Whenever there is a puberty ceremony for girls, The People usually mold and shape the young lady in the likeness of some respected and beautiful person. This is done according to the Sun's order.

After the two boys were molded and shaped like their half brother, they were fed. Then the Sun asked them, "Now what do you want?" He opened the door to the east and showed the boys all kinds of precious things, "This?"

"No," replied the boys. "We did not come for those things. They are beautiful and valuable, but we did not come for those."

The Sun then opened the door to the south and asked, "Those?" He opened the doors to the west and to the north, but the boys refused all. At one of the doors he showed them horses, and, at another, he showed all kinds of jewels. The Sun knew what the boys were after. He knew they wanted weapons with which to rid the earth of all the monsters.

Then the boys spoke up, "One thing we came for, Father — a weapon to kill all the monsters roaming our land. We must kill the monsters, because they are endangering every single person in our land. People cannot increase in numbers because they are being killed by these terrible monsters."

The sun sat there for a while and thought it over. Finally, he said, "I hate to do it, because many of those monsters are my own offspring."

The boys pointed out the weapons they wanted, "We want that bow and arrow," they said. The bow and arrow happened to be made of thunder and

Asdzą́ą́ Nádleehé (Changing Woman)

lightning. The Sun did not want them to have it because it was so powerful and could kill the monsters, but he finally agreed to give them the weapons they requested. The Sun said, "All right, my children, I will let you use the weapons, but I will not let you keep them. After you get through with them return them to me. When you bring them back, I will give you a substitute for them. Now, I will take you back to the center of the sky and release you from there. But, the first monster you want to kill, the lonely roaming giant, is your brother. He is my son, so I will do the killing. I will kill him myself."

They left with their father early in the morning on their journey across the sky. When they arrived above the center of the earth, which was at Mount Taylor, the Sun gave them another test. He asked them to identify various places all over the surface of the earth. He asked, "Where is your home?" The boys knew where their home was. They pointed out Huerfano Mountain and said that was where they lived. The Sun next asked, "What mountain is that in the East?"

"That's *Sis Naajiní* (Blanca Peak)," replied the boys.

"What mountain is down here below us?"

"That's *Tsoodził* (Mount Taylor)," said the boys.

"What mountain is that in the West?"

"That's *Dook'o'oosłíí́d* (San Francisco Peak)."

"Now, what mountain is that over in the north?"

"Those are the *Dibé Nitsaa* (La Plata Mountains)."

Because all the boys' answers were correct, the Sun said goodby to them as they were lowered down to the earth at the place called *Tó Sidoh* (Hot Springs).

La Plata Mountains in Colorado

Dibé Nitsaa

San Francisco Peak,
near Flagstaff, Arizona

Dook'o'oosłííd

Mount Taylor in New Mexico   Tsoodził

Chapter 6

Killing the Monsters

THE FIRST MONSTER THE TWINS set out to kill, upon their return from their visit to the Sun, was *Yé'iitsoh Łá'í Naagháii* (One Walking Giant). The Monster lived at *Tó Sidoh* (Hot Springs). The Twins waited near the lake for him to come and drink. The older brother went to the east side, overlooking the lake, and waited for *Yé'iitsoh*. Some time passed before the older Twin saw the giant *Yé'ii's* head sticking out from nearby. It was obvious that *Yé'iitsoh* was being careful about his approach to the lake. Next *Yé'iitsoh* walked over to the south side and from there one of the Twins could see to the waist of the giant. Then *Yé'iitsoh* moved to the west side where he became visible to the knees. Finally, *Yé'iitsoh* approached from the north and went to the lake and drank four times. He drank all the water and then spit it back, and the lake was as it was before.

Yé'iitsoh stood up and saw the boys. He said, "What are the beautiful two things I see? How shall I kill them?"

The Twins answered back, "What is the beautiful big thing we see? How shall we kill it?" They called to each other four times. Then the messenger warned the Twins that *Yé'iitsoh* was going to shoot his arrows. The Twins stood on their feathers, and, when *Yé'iitsoh* shot, the feathers lifted the Twins out of the path of the arrow. Four times *Yé'iitsoh* tried to hit the Twins with his arrows and each time the boys were able to get out of the way. The Sun had told the Twins they must wait for *Yé'iitsoh* to act first since the monster was the oldest.

When the Twins' turn came there was a blinding flash of lightning which struck *Yé'iitsoh*, but the giant just stood there and did not fall. Then the Twins threw their knives at him. When they hit *Yé'iitsoh* with their last weapon he fell with a terrible noise, and when he hit the earth it shook. Blood began to flow from *Yé'iitsoh*, and the messenger warned the Twins not to let the blood join together or the monster would come back to life. The Twins prevented the blood from coming together. They collected the reward of the tail feather the Sun had requested plus *Yé'iitsoh's* skull which later caused Monster Slayer's illness.

Then the Twins returned to their mother's hogan and told her where they had been and that they had killed *Yé'iitsoh*. At first, Changing Woman did not believe them, but later she did.

Killing one of the monsters – the Giant.

When the Twins hit *Yé'iitsoh* (Yei Tso) with their last weapon he fell with a loud noise, shaking the earth.

Killing the Monsters

Today one can see the dried blood of *Yé'iitsoh* near Grants, New Mexico. The place is called the lava beds by white people.

Now, Monster Slayer set out in search of *Tsédahódzííłtáłii* (the Monster That Kicked People Off the Cliff). He was a monster in human form who appeared harmless and pleasant. He just lay beside the narrow path in the shade. He Who Kicked People Off the Cliff lived in the Mesa Verde area at a place called Wild Horse Mesa. When Monster Slayer found this Being he asked, "Grandfather, is it all right to pass through here?" The monster answered, "Yes, people pass back and forth through here." Monster Slayer pretended to take a step forward but drew back very quickly. The monster kicked and missed. Monster Slayer said, "What does that mean, Grandfather?"

He Who Kicked People Off the Cliff replied, "Oh, I had a bad cramp in my leg." The same thing happened four times; then Monster Slayer hit the monster with his knife and killed him. He found that his hair had grown into the cleft in the rock like the roots of a tree. Monster Slayer cut the hair and the body fell down below.

Next Monster Slayer went hunting the monster that tore up the ground with his horns, *Déélgééd*. Child Born of Water was to remain home and watch the firebrand and prayer sticks. Monster Slayer said, "When you see one of the medicine sticks start to burn you will know that the monster is getting the best of me. Take the medicine stick in your hand and draw smoke from it into your mouth. Then blow the smoke on the prayer sticks and toward the four directions. This will give me new strength."

The Horned Monster had excellent eyesight, and, whenever he saw a person, he would charge and eat that person alive. Monster Slayer found where the Horned Monster was living and crept close, through a bunch of tall grass. The animal was large, with hair like a moose and a great pair of horns that stood high in the air. Monster Slayer could not crawl close enough to the Horned Monster.

Just as Monster Slayer was losing hope of getting close enough, Gopher came by and asked what he wanted. Monster Slayer said, "Grandmother, I am trying to get as near as possible to the Horned Monster so that I can kill him." The *Na'azísí* (Gopher) agreed to help, and she dug a tunnel leading right under the monster's heart. The monster was covered with hair which was so thick that an arrow would not penetrate. In order to help, Gopher chewed off the hair over the heart of the Horned Monster.

Monster Slayer used his lightning arrow and killed the Horned Monster. Then *Hazéíts'ósii* (Chipmunk) climbed up on the horns of the monster to see if he really was dead. He wiped the blood from the animal's mouth on his back from his head to his tail. That is why Chipmunk has dark lines running the length of his back today. Gopher took some of the blood and rubbed it over her hands and her face. That is why gophers have dark faces.

Then Monster Slayer returned to the hogan of his mother, Changing Woman, and told her he had killed the Horned Monster. Again Changing Woman did not believe it, but he showed her the hide of the monster; so she believed him.

Monster Slayer searched for, and found, Monster That Kicked People Off the Cliff — *Tsédahódzííłtáłii*.

Monster Slayer killed the Horned Monster with his lightning arrow.

Killing the Monsters

Now Monster Slayer set out to kill *Tsé Nináhálééh* (Monster Bird). The giant killer bird and his family lived on top of Shiprock. Monster Slayer wore the hideskin coat of the Horned Monster, and around his neck he wore some of the blood vessels from that monster, as well as a part of the horn itself. Also, he placed two sacred feathers under his arms. Then he walked about making himself conspicuous to the Monster Bird. Pretty soon he heard a swishing sound from above and the giant bird swooped down and picked him up and carried him to *Tsé Bit'a'í* (Rock With Wings). The Monster Bird dropped him into the nest from a great height. Monster Slayer landed without harm with the help of his sacred feathers and the Horned Monster's horn. He lay in the nest and cut open the blood vessels that he carried around his neck so that it would look as though he had been killed from the fall. The Monster Bird called to his two young children who were in the nest and told them to eat. When the young birds approached Monster Slayer he chased them away. The two young birds began to cry, but Monster Slayer told them to be quiet and he would not hurt them. He asked when their father would return and the children said, "When the Male Rain begins to fall." Later, Male Rain began to fall, and the father giant bird flew into the nest. Monster Slayer was ready and killed him with his arrow.

Later, when the Female Rain began to fall, the mother Monster Bird returned to the nest, and Monster Slayer killed her in like manner.

True to his word, Monster Slayer did not harm the two young birds. He told the older of the two birds, "From now on you must not think as your father thought. The *Diné* shall use you, your claws, your feathers and other parts." After listening to Monster Slayer the bird rose and flew up into the sky. This bird became the *Atsá* (Eagle).

Next, Monster Slayer spoke to the younger bird in the same manner. The younger bird then flew away. He became the *Na'ashjaa'* (Owl).

After that, Monster Slayer tried to find a way to get down from the nest perched on the top of Shiprock. He barely could make out features on the ground below.

He saw an old woman walking beneath Shiprock. Monster Slayer called and asked for help. At first the old woman was afraid, but finally she agreed to help. The old woman, who was Spider Woman, got her basket, and, after warning Monster Slayer not to open his eyes during the descent, she successfully lowered him to safety. In return, she was allowed to keep the feathers from the wings and tail of the Monster Bird.

Then Monster Slayer returned to the home of Changing Woman, where he announced that he had killed the Bird Monsters.

Monster Slayer, with the help of his younger brother, Child Born of Water, killed the remaining monsters, including *Bináá'yee Aghánii* (Eyes That Kill), *Jádí Naakits'áadah Naajeehii* (Twelve Running Antelopes) and *Tsé Naagháii* (Rolling Rock).

The older of the two birds became an eagle.　　　　　　　　　　　　　　　　　　　　Atsá

Yei Tso's Blood south of Mt. Taylor, New Mexico

Yé'ii Tsoh Bidił

Next, Monster Slayer decided to kill the Monster Bird — *Tsé Nináháléééh* — which lived with its family on the top of Shiprock.

Killing the Monsters

After Monster Slayer and Child Born of Water had killed the terrible and destructive monsters in their homeland, they were resting when they saw a red flare coming from a distance. "I wonder who is still alive over there, where the red flare is coming from," said one of the Twins.

The other Twin said, "Let us go see."

They walked and walked a great distance. Finally, they came to a place where smoke was coming up from the earth. They peeked down through a hole and saw old people resting in a room below.

Quietly they found a doorway and entered the room and found many kinds of monsters. "Here is another monster," said one of the Twins. "Let's kill him."

The old man lifted his head and said, "Grandsons! Why would you kill me? I am *Dichin Hastiih* (Hunger). How are people going to live in the future without me? Would you have them eating just one meal forever? There will be new food to eat and taste whenever people are hungry. People are born with openings for the taking in and giving out of food. Is that not so?"

"We will spare your life," said one of the Twins. "I can see that you may be useful in the future."

"But here is another one we can kill," said the other Twin. "Look at him. He is a hideous old creature and surely must be a monster of destruction."

"You cannot kill me, Grandson," said this old man. "You must let me live for I am *Tę'é'į́ Hastiih* (Poverty). Clothes must be worn out. Moccasins must someday have holes in their soles. You see I can be useful. If old things did not wear out there would be no reason for making new ones."

"He is right," said the twin who was about to kill him. "I suppose we must let him live, but over there is another who seems already dead. If he is not, we can kill him."

The other Twin lifted his club, but let it rest on the old man who lay there with his eyes closed. He opened his eyes and looked up at the young man. He saw the club and knew what the Twin was about to do.

"No! Wait! You must not kill me." He said, "I am *Bił Hastiih* (Sleep). Who could be more useful than I am? People need me when they are ill or tired. I am able to restore their energy and even their lives. I beg you not to kill me." So his life also was spared, because the Twins realized how useful sleep could be. How terrible a place the earth would be if people could not sometimes forget their troubles and go to sleep.

Only two dreadful-looking old creatures were left in the room. "There is still one for each of us to kill," said a Twin. "Which do you choose?"

"I'll take this one," said the other Twin, pointing to a bony old man who was crawling with lice. "I think we should kill him and get him out of the way."

The old man sat up and begged, "Spare me. Please spare me. I am the *Yaa' Hastiih* (Lice Man) who gets in people's hair if they do not keep clean. People need me to remind them to keep clean. When they have nothing else to do they can kill

The Twins were tempted to get rid of such things as Hunger, Poverty, Sleep, Lice Man and Old Age; but all of these things pleaded to be allowed to exist, and the Twins consented.

Killing the Monsters

little parts of me with their finger nails. People should have something to remind them to keep their hair and bodies clean." The Twins agreed and lowered their clubs.

"That leaves only this one for me to kill," said the other Twin. "What will his plea be?"

"My plea?" the old man asked. "I am *Sá* (Old Age), Grandson. Let there be old age so people can die while others are being born. Let people reach old age and still live a few more years. Do not kill them when they are still useful."

"Shall we listen to him?" asked the Twin who was about to crush the old man's skull with his club.

"Yes," said his brother. "I guess there always must be young people and old people." After listening to the old man, the boys spared his life.

Today people eat to nourish their bodies and are interested each day in food; they make shoes and clothing and wear them out; they enjoy sleep when they are tired; they keep clean to live more comfortably, and babies are being born daily while older people are closing their eyes forever in death.

After destroying the monsters and allowing old age, hunger and others to live, Monster Slayer and Child Born of Water climbed the four sacred mountains and looked about in four directions. They saw no monsters, and they decided that at last there were no more monsters to kill and destroy mankind.

Then the Twins returned to their home at *Dził Ná'oodiłii* (Huerfano Mountain) where their mother, Changing Woman, lived.

The Twins told her that their work was finished. All the monsters that harmed people had been slain. *Naayéé' Nééezghání* (Monster Slayer) took off his armor and lay down his knives and his lightning weapon which the Sun had given him. Then the Sun came and said, "My son, it is well now. I shall take my weapons back with me."

The Twins returned certain weapons to their father, the Sun, as they had agreed to do. The zigzag lightning arrow, the straight lightning arrow, the rainbow arrow, the dark flint club, the blue flint club, the yellow flint club, the serrated flint club and all of the flint armor the Twins returned to their father. They kept the sun ray arrow and their sun ray means to travel.

After all the monsters had been killed, Monster Slayer and Child Born of Water decided they wanted to visit the home of their father once again.[1] They remembered all the other good things the Sun had shown them on their trip to his

---

1
Some Navajo versions do not mention a second visit to the Sun.

They returned most of the weapons to their father, the Sun, as they had agreed to do. The zigzag lightning arrow, the straight lightning arrow, the rainbow arrow, the dark flint club, the blue flint club, the yellow flint club, the serrated flint club and the flint armor — all of these the Twins gave back to their father.

Killing the Monsters

home. The Sun welcomed them and asked the purpose of the trip. The Twins told the Sun how all the monsters had been killed; but the Sun, of course, already knew about it.

Next, Monster Slayer and Child Born of Water said, "When we were here before you showed us four rooms filled with horses, sheep, cattle, corn and seeds. Now, we have come for those things."

The Sun replied, "My children, you ask for too much. The last time you chose not to accept these things. You chose the weapons to use to kill the Monsters. Some of these were my own children. I sacrificed my own children at your request. This time I will not give you your request unless you grant me my wish."

The Twins asked, "What is it you want from us?"

The Sun answered, "You must allow me to destroy those who live in houses."

After a great deal of thought the Twins agreed to the bargain.

The Sun then gave to Monster Slayer and Child Born of Water obsidian, turquoise, abalone and white shell horses from the east; elk, antelopes, porcupines, deer and rabbits from the south; white, blue, yellow and black corn, striped and varicolored corn, as well as pollen from the west, and other plants and small birds from the north.

In addition, the Sun gave to the Twins rainbow, zigzag lightning and sun ray from the east; mirages from the south; he-rain and she-rain from the west, and dark and white mist from the north.

Monster Slayer and Child Born of Water returned to their home with the gifts from the Sun. After four days the Sun arrived to carry out the other part of the agreement. However, the Holy People had picked up a man and a woman and pairs of all animals to save before the Sun began his destruction. The Sun put Big Yellow Hail into the Pine Stick, Big Blue Hail into the Spruce Stick, Big White Hail into the Oak and Big Black Hail into the small Oak stick. A whirlwind arose and rains came down. A flood covered the earth, destroying a great deal.

Finally, the waters went down and the Holy People put back those whom they had saved.

After that, Monster Slayer became very tired and concerned. He felt distressed and lacked peace and harmony.[2] One day he was found unconscious and bloody. He had been almost beaten to death. Child Born of Water came and saw the terrible condition his brother was in. There was evidence that the attackers had spat on Monster Slayer and had made fun of him. Witnesses said the assailants had made fun of his deeds. The attackers would say, "So this is the famous Monster Slayer," and then hit him with sticks.[3]

The people held a meeting to decide how to help Monster Slayer. The raven was at this meeting, along with others whose help was needed. It is from this incident that the first Squaw Dance came. This ceremony was performed over Monster Slayer, and he recovered.

---

[2]
Yé'iitsoh's skull had affected him psychologically.

[3]
This part of the story is not included in many versions.

An *agháá³* (prayer stick), used during the first Squaw Dance to cure Monster Slayer.

Chapter 7

Origin of the Clans

AFTER CHANGING WOMAN HAD TAUGHT and helped the people (animals) living within the four Sacred Mountains, and after all the monsters were killed, the Sun wanted her to come and live with him. He promised to build a beautiful home in the Western Ocean just for her. Changing Woman did not want to leave the land and the people she loved. Finally, the Sun and the Twins, her sons, convinced her it would be best to move to a new home in the west. In order that Changing Woman would not be lonesome, some of the people decided to go with her to her new home.

These people (animals) lived with her in the west for some time, but later they became lonely as they heard of people like themselves who still lived in their old homeland. Finally, they decided to return. Changing Woman thought that there should be more people, so she created more of them (humans) by rubbing the skin from her breast, from her back and from under both arms. In this way she created the first four clans. Changing Woman rubbed the skin from her breast and formed people who became the *Kiiyaa'áanii* clan. From the skin rubbed from her back the *Honágháahnii* clan was formed. From the skin under her right arm the *Tó Dích'íi'nii* clan was created, and from the skin under her left arm the *Hashtł'ishnii* clan was made.

When they left the west, Changing Woman gave each of the four clans an animal pet as a guardian. A head man for the *Kiiyaa'áanii* (Towering House) clan had been given a *Shash* (bear) for protection. The *Honágháahnii* (One Walks Around You) clan was given a *Nashdóí* (lion). Another, who was to be the first member of the *Tó Dích'íi'nii* (Bitter Water) clan, was given a *Tł'iish Tsoh* (bull snake). The human to be the first member of the *Hashtł'ishnii* (Mud) clan was given a *Dahsání* (porcupine).

With their animals, the four groups left for their land in the east. They first went to *Dook'o'oosłííd* (San Francisco Peak). They were accompanied by *Haashch'ééłti'í* (Talking God) and *Haashch'ééhwaan* (Second Talking God), who made the first sacrifice of *Nitł'is* (precious stone) on the summit.

The Sun caused a wonderful home to be built on an island in the Western Ocean for Changing Woman. It was made of rock crystal which shined brightly and reflected beautiful rainbows.

In this way, from various parts of her body, Changing Woman created the first four clans.

When they left the west, Changing Woman gave each of the four clans an animal pet. One head man was given a bear for protection. Another received a lion.

Origin of the Clans

The journey back from the west took place magically until they got to *Tsin Béél'áhí* (Tree Grove Slope — Bill Williams Mountains). From there the humans had to travel on their own, as their sacred means of transportation, *Shándíín* (sun rays), *Níłtsą́* (rain trails), *Shábitł'óól* (sunbeams), and other means of transportation provided by the Holy People, were finished.

The humans continued on their own from there to the place called *Dził Bi'áadii* (Female Mountain), where they found a corn plant in their path. Two of the people ran over to the corn and one of them broke off the bottom ear of corn and the other broke off the top ear.

The ear of corn from the top was white and the one from the bottom was yellow. The corn stalk was taken out of the ground, placed on a piece of *naak'ą'dithił* (black cotton material) and covered with *naak'ą'ałgaii* (white cotton material), and a chant was performed over the cornstalk.

From the stalk rose two men and two women to join the members of the first four clans, and the band continued the journey. As the humans were about to descend the trail at *Naanaz'áii* (Corner of Mountain), they heard laughter from over the hill. As the party drew closer, they saw a large dwelling. As they approached, the dwelling the laughter ceased. Two people went to the dwelling to investigate.

They walked inside and found no one, but a fire was burning. Then they noticed a *Nashdóí kágí* (lion skin) quiver hanging on the east wall. On the other walls were quivers of *Tábaastíín* (otter skin), *Hashdółtbéí* (bobcat skin) and a *Tseełgaii* (many white tails).

From these quivers were to emerge enemies of the Navajos. The two humans inside the dwelling wondered out loud, "Where is everybody?"

Suddenly, a sound came from within the quiver on the east wall, and a *K'aa'* (arrow) fell out onto the floor. From it a young man arose. This happened with each quiver. One of the four young men said, "This place is not for land-walking people. Leave here immediately."

The two humans hurried out of the dwelling, not waiting to find out who those men were. Rejoining the group, the two humans continued on their journey to *Dził Yíjiin* (Black Mountain), where they crossed a river at Rocky Crossing and then made camp in the forest for the night.

Everyone bedded down shortly after passing over the river. Near dawn, a chant was heard from the east where the bear was lying. Then the Navajos were attacked by the *K'aa' Dine'é* (Many Arrows People). These were the ones from the *Tseełgaii* (many white tails) quiver back at the dwelling they had stopped to investigate.

The situation was desperate, and only the help of the animal guardians given by Changing Woman prevented the Navajos from being overwhelmed. The bear and the lion raced back and forth, and the porcupine shot his quills in all directions. The bull snake was using *Tł'iish K'aa'* (Arrow Snake) as a weapon.

The wandering Navajos were attacked by the *K'aa' Dine'é* (Many Arrows People), and a bitter fight followed.

Origin of the Clans

"What is the enemy trying to do?" asked the bull snake. In order to help further, he rubbed two rocks together to create a fire which blazed through the forest. The trees burned down, leaving part of *Dził Yíjiin* (Black Mountain) bare, as it is to this day.

The journey continued from *Dził Yíjiin* to *Bą̨ąh Tóii* (Water on It) and on to *Tó Naneesdizí* (Tuba City). The people became thirsty in this arid country where there was no possibility of finding water. They saw many *k'aa béésh* (stone flints) as they passed through.

One person said to another one who was carrying *yoołgai gish* (white shell cane), "We were to use that cane whenever we were in need of something. Now we need water. We must use the cane." (At the creation of the four clans, each clan had been given a cane.)

The person carrying the cane stuck it into the ground and up gushed water. They decided then that this well never would overflow nor dry up. To this day, it remains at the same level, as it has for many years.

The people spent the night nearby before continuing on to *Naashdóíts'į'ǫ́* (on the east side of Black Mountain). There the person carrying the *dootl'izhii gish* (turquoise cane) stuck it into a crevice in the rocks and, again, water poured forth.

The people moved to *Tó Nahalį́į́h* (Tonalea). A little way south from there were two pillars of rock. The people turned to the person carrying the *bááshzhinii gish* (obsidian stone cane) and said, "We are thirsty, see what you can do to get some water." So this person stuck his cane into the ground. Instead of water, mud gushed out. To this day, there is a muddy water hole there, where many livestock die after being trapped by quicksand.

From there the people moved to *Tsé Ani'įihí* (Thief Rock), then to *Téé' Nidééh* (Where Things Fall Into a Canyon), and on to *Aghaah Łá* (Much Wool, El Capitan).

Back at *Dził Yíjiin*, the bear had been turned loose for rear guard duty.

The lion was freed at *Naashdóíts'į'ǫ́* to guard against any intruders or anyone pursuing the people.

Only the porcupine and the bull snake remained with the group. They moved to *Tsin Bideez'á* (Wooded Mesa) and across to *Dziłna'neests'ee'ii* (Mountainous Region). There the bull snake said, "I am tired of my load, Grandchildren." He was released there, and, to this day, many of his descendants still can be found there.

Now only the porcupine was traveling with the group to *Dził K'ih Hózhǫnii* (Beautiful Mountain). At that spot the porcupine finally left the group.

From there, the people went back to a place below the northwest point of *Lók'aa'yigai* (Lukachukai Mountains), at *Dá'ák'ehalání* (Large Cultivated Fields). At that time, however, the people grew tired of the long journey and turned back.

As soon as they changed the direction of their travel, Changing Woman disapproved. She instructed *Haashch'éełti'í* (Talking God of the White Shell People) and *Dootł'izhii Dine'é* (of the Turquoise People), "Have a *Hozhǫ́ǫ́jí* (Blessing Way Ceremony) for my people at these places: *Tsin Béél'áhí* (Tree Grove, Bill Williams

Black Mountain in Arizona (as seen from Rough Rock, where the Navajo Curriculum Center is located at the Rough Rock Demonstration School)

Dził Yíjiin

Origin of the Clans

Mountains); at *Hajíínéí* (Place of Emergence); at *Ch'óol'į́į́* (Gobernador Knob); at *Dził Ná'ooditii* (Huerfano Mountain), and at *Sis Naat'eel* (Wide Belt Mesa). Have Blessing Way Ceremonies for the people at all these places. Then, maybe they will not turn back again. They must have the ceremony."

Haashch'éełti'í and *Dootł'izhii Dine'é* went to all the locations mentioned and arranged for a ceremony to be held at each place. They determined who was to perform each ceremony.

In the evening, White Shell Woman (Changing Woman) told the two to see if the ceremonies were being performed; so they went from one spot to another until they came to the last place. When they arrived, the Hogan Songs were being sung. *Haashch'éełti'í* (Talking God of the White Shell People) and his partner were told, "What's going on, you two? Sing us a song. You two are just running around."

They both agreed to sing their songs, and, after doing so, they left for their own homes.

When the two messengers returned, Changing Woman asked them if they had brought back the canes from the ceremonies, and they replied, "We left them there." Changing Woman exclaimed: "What do you mean, you left them there? Why? You two have erred. Go back and repeat everything."

It is because of this mistake that the six parts of the Blessing Way Ceremony were doubled to become twelve parts. Later, one more part was added to make thirteen.

In those days the Holy People were very close to the Navajos, and many times they actually visited and taught them. Through these teachings the power and the beauty of the Holy People became known to the Navajos, and, as a result, they increased and prospered.

Under the guidance and protection of the Holy People many more Navajo clans came into existence, and the small handful of people who had come into the Fourth World, even with the creation of the four clans by Changing Woman, grew and grew, until today one can speak properly and with pride of the Navajo Nation.

Chapter 8

Division of the People

MOST OF THE PEOPLE started moving around from place to place. As they moved around, they left one group, *Béíyóodzin* (the Paiutes), in the *Naatsis'áá* (Navajo Mountain area) because of differences over religious matters. From this area, the main group moved down toward the south, where they left the *Chíshí* (Chiricahua Apaches). Then they went to the east, where the *Naashgalí Diné'é* (Mescalero Apaches) decided to stay. These Mescaleros now live from Albuquerque all the way down to the home of the *Naakaii* (Mexicans). From there, the people again moved to the vicinity of *Dibé Nitsaa* (La Plata Mountains), where the *Beehai* (Jicarilla Apaches) eventually settled. The People remained there for seven winters. They were happy, but there was one problem. The summers were too short. Because there was not time for the squash and corn to ripen, the main group moved to *Tsé Naajiin* (Cabezon Peak).

The home of The People eventually existed within the boundaries of the four sacred mountains. The names of these mountains were decided upon by *Haashch'ééh Diné'é* (Holy People), and one god was left within each of these mountains. That is why they are sacred to this day. Eight more smaller mountains also are holy.

There is a *Yé'ii* (God) whose body starts at the foot of *Tsoodził* (Mount Taylor) and curves all the way around on the outside of the four Sacred Mountains, with the head stopping at *Sis Naajiní* (Blanca Peak). This was done to give The People protection. When the population increases so much that The People spread out beyond the boundary represented by the God's body, that will be the end of the Navajos. Because Navajo people live beyond that boundary now, it could be that they will run into difficulties with nature and will be out of harmony with the plan of the Gods.

Round Rock, between Many Farms and the community of Round Rock in Arizona Tsé Nikání

Beautiful Mountain in New Mexico, southwest of Shiprock Dził K'ih Hózhónii

Cabezon Peak in New Mexico

Tsé Naajiin

Navajo Mountain, southern Utah *Naatsis'áá*

Bahlaki Mesa, south of Salina, Arizona   Báálók'aa'í

Fish Point, at south end
of Black Mountain in Arizona

Łóó' Háálį́

GLOSSARY

Aghaah Łá	Much Wool — El Capitan
Aghááł	Prayer Stick
Ak'i Dah Nást'ání	Hosta Butte, near Crownpoint, New Mexico
Álílee	Through a miraculous power
Ałch'į' adeez'á	Male hogan
Ałtsé Asdzą́ą́	First Woman
Ałtsé Hashké	First Scolder
Ałtsé Hastiin	First Man
Ánít'į́į́h	Poison
Asdzą́ą́ Nádleehé	Changing Woman
Atsá	Eagle
Atsiniłtl'ish	Lightning
Atsiniltł'ish k'aa'	Lightning That Strikes Crooked.
Bąąh Tóii	Water on It
Báálók'aa'í	Bahlaki Mesa, south of Salina, Arizona
Bááshzhinii At'ééd	Obsidian Girl
Bááshzhinii gish	Obsidian stone cane
Beehai	Jicarilla Apaches
Béésh doolghasii	Flint knives
Beiyóodzin	The Paiutes
Bįįh	Deer
Bił Hastiih	Sleep
Bináá'yee Agháníi	Monster That Killed With His Eyes
Bi yeel	Sacrifice
Ch'idí	Buffalo hide — blanket
Chíshí	Chiricahua Apaches
Ch'óol'į́'į́	Precious Stones — Gobernador Knob in New Mexico
Dá'ák'ehalání	Large Cultivated Fields — Many Farms
Dah na'aghízii	Pouch
Dahs'aní	Porcupine
Déélgééd	Horned Monster
Dibé Nitsaa	Obsidian Mountain — La Plata Mountains
Dibé Shijé'é	Sheep Hill Mountain, near Flagstaff, Arizona

Fortified Mesa, eastern side of San Mateo Mountains in New Mexico   Yoo' Tsoh

Glossary

Dichin Hastiih	Hunger
Diichiłí Askii	Abalone Shell Boy
Dilyéhé	Seven Stars
Dloziłgai	Squirrels
Diné	People (the Navajo people)
Dólii	Blue Bird
Doo Honoot'ínii	Name of first seed corn
Dook'o'oosłííd	Abalone Shell Mountain — San Francisco Peak
Dootł'iizhii Askii	Turquoise Boy
Dootł'izhii At'ééd	Turquoise Girl
Dootł'izhii Dine'é	Turquoise People
Dootł'izhii gish	Turquoise cane
Dził Bi'áadii	Female Mountain
Dził Dah Neezłínii	Roof Butte, Lukachukai Mountains, Arizona
Dził K'ih Hózhónii	Beautiful Mountain
Dziłłeezh	Mountain dirt
Dził Náhoozłii	Carrizo Mountains in Arizona
Dzil Naajinii	Sleeping Ute Mountain, near Cortez, Colorado
Dził na'neests'ee'ii	Mountain region
Dził Ná'oodiłii	Banded Rock Mountain — Huerfano Mountain in New Mexico
Dził Yíjiin	Black Mountain, Arizona
Gáagii	Crow
Ginítsoh Dootł'izh	Blue Hawks
Haashch'ééh Dine'é	The Holy People
Haashch'éełti'í	Talking God
Haashch'ééhwaan	Second Talking God
Haashch'ééshzhiní	Black God
Haashch'éewaan	House of Talking God
Hadahoniiye'bee Hooghan	House Made of Banded Rock
Hajíínéí	Place of Emergence
Hashdóiłbéí	Bobcat skin
Hashtł'ishnii	Mud Clan
Hatsoo'algha K'aa'	Lightning That Flashes Straight
Hazéíts'ósii	Chipmunk
Hiinááh bits'os	Magic eagle feather
Honágháahnii	One Walks Around You Clan
Honeeshjish	First Poker
Hooghan nímazí	Female hogan
Hózhǫ́ǫ́jí	Blessing Way Ceremony
Ii'ni'bika'ii	Big Thunder — Male Lightning
Jaa'abaní	Bat People

Roof Butte, Lukachukai Mountains, Arizona

Dzil Dah Neezłínii

Tsaile Butte (Peak), Chuska Mountains, Arizona

Tsézhin Dits'in

Jádí Naakits'áadah Naajeehii	Twelve Running Antelopes
Jádí Naakits'áadah Náhiníléíi	Twelve Antelopes
Jóhónaa'éí	The Sun
Jóhónaa'éí Hataa'lá	Twins' Father (the Sun)
Joogii	Blue Jays
K'aa'	Arrow
K'aa béésh	Stone flints
K'aa' Dine'é	Many Arrows People (Clan)
K'eet'áán	Wand
K'et'ą́ą́z	Yucca counters
Kiiyaa'ą́ąnii	Tower House Clan
Kinaaldá	Walked into Beauty
Kiníí' Na'ígai	White House Ruin, Canyon de Chelly, Arizona
K'os diłhił	Black cloud
Lók'áá' Adigishii	Reeds That Cut
Lók'aa'yigai	Lukachukai Mountains
Łók'aa'	White Reeds
Łóó' Háálį́	Fish Point, south end of Black Mountain in Arizona
Ma'iiłtsóí	Kit Foxes
Mą'iitsoh	Wolves
Mósí	Cat People
Naak'ą'ałgaii	White cotton material
Naak'ą'diłhił	Black cotton material
Naakaii	Mexicans
Naanaz'áii	Corner of Mountain
Naashdóíłbéí	Bobcat skin
Naashdóíts'į'ǫ́	East side of Black Mountain
Naashgalí Dine'é	Mescalero Apaches
Na'ashjaa'	Owl
Na'ashjé'ii	Spider People
Na'ashjé'ii Asdzą́ą́	Spider Woman
Na'ashjé'ii Hastiin	Spider Man
Naashkǫ́ǫ́'	Raft
Na'ashǫ́'ii	Snakes
Na'ashǫ́'iiłbáhí	Lizards
Naatsis'ą́	Navajo Mountain areas
Na'ats'ǫǫsí	Mice
Naayéé'	Monster
Naayéé' Neezghání	Monster Slayer
Na'azísí	Gopher
Na'azǫ́zii	Spider Ant

Man and Woman Turned to Stone,
near Rock Point, Arizona

Tsé Ahíʾ Halní'í

Spider Rock, Canyon de Chelly, Arizona   Tsé Na'ashjé'ii

Mountain, White Cone, near Wheatfields, Arizona,
where incest medicine plants are found. Wheatfields
Lake is in the foreground.   Séí heets'ózii

Glossary

Nádleeh	The Hermaphrodite
Nahashch'id	Badger
Nahodits'ǫ'	Wash That Swallowed
Náhookǫs	Big Dipper
Náhookǫs	Little Dipper
Nashdóí	Lion
Nashdóí kágí	Lion skin
Náshdóílbéí	Wildcats
Náshdóítsoh	Mountain Lions
Nihodeeshgiizh Ch'ínílíní	Pueblo Pintado in New Mexico
Níłch'i Diłhił	Black Wind
Níłtsą	Rain trails
Níłtsągo'	Beetles
Nitł'is	Precious stone
Níyoltsoh	Big Wind — tornado
Nohodeetł'iish	Blue cloud
Są́	Old Age
Séí heets'ózii	White Cone, near Wheatfields, Arizona
Séít'áád	Moving Sand
Shábitł'óól	Sunbeams
Shándíín	Sun rays
Shash	Bear
Shash Na'ałkaahii	Tracking Bear
Shashtsoh	A huge bear
Sis Naajiní	Dawn, or White Shell Mountain (Blanca Peak)
Sis Naat'eel	Wide Belt Mesa
Sǫ' Doo Nídízídí	Morning Star
Sǫ'tsoh	North Star
Tábaastíín	Otter skin
Táchééh	First sweat bath
Tadzootse'	Black Rock
Tátłkáá' Dijádii	Water Skeeter
Tátłł'áái Ha'alééh	Blue Herons
Tániil'áii	Dragon Flies
Tązhii	Turkeys
Tééhoołtsódii	Water Monster
Tééhoołtsódii Biyázhí	Water Monster's baby
Té'é'į́ Hastiih	Poverty
Téé' Nidééh	Where Things Fall into a Canyon
Tl'éhonaa'éí	Moon
Tł'iish	Snake

Los Gigantes Buttes, near Round Rock, Arizona 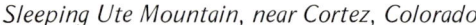 *Tsé Áłts'óóz íí'áhí*

Sleeping Ute Mountain, near Cortez, Colorado  *Dził Naajinii*

Glossary

Tł'iish K'aa'	Arrow Snake
Tł'iish Tsoh	Bull Snake
Tł'iish tsoh Dooniniti'ii	Gigantic Snake
Tó ádin Dah Azką	Waterless Mountain, west of Chinle, Arizona
Tó Aheedlí	Where the Rivers Cross (Navajo Lake, New Mexico)
Tó Ałnáozlí	Crossing of the Waters
Tó Bájísh Chíní	Child Born of Water
Tó Bił Dahisk'id	Place Where the Waters Crossed
Tó Dích'íi'nii	Bitter Water Clan
Tódiłhił	Black Water Lake
Tólásht'óshí	Ball (for shoe games)
Tó Naneesdizí	Tuba City, Arizona
Tó Nahalííh	Tonalea, Arizona
Tó Niłchoní	Stinking Lake, near El Vado, New Mexico
Tó Sidoh	Hot Springs
Tsé' Ahéenínidił	Canyon Which Closed in on a Traveler
Tsé' Ahéénídiłii	Crushing Rock
Tsé Ahił Halni'í	Man and Woman Turned to Stone (near Rock Point, Arizona)
Tsé Ałts'óózíí'áhí	Los Gigantes Buttes (near Round Rock, Arizona)
Tsé Ani'įįhí	Thief Rock
Tsé Bit'a'í	Rock with Wings — Shiprock
Tsé Biyah Anii'áhí	Pueblo Bonito, Chaco Canyon in New Mexico
Tsédahódzíłtáłii	Monster That Kicked People Off the Cliff
Tseełgaii	Many White Tails
Tségháhoodzání	Window Rock, at capital of Navajo Nation, Window Rock, Arizona.
Tsé'íí'áhá	The Fingers
Tséłchííyi'	Red Rock
Tsé Naagháii	Rolling Rock
Tsé Na'ashjé'ii	Spider Rock, Canyon de Chelly, Arizona
Tsé Naajiin	Cabezon Peak
Tsé Nikání	Round Rock, between Many Farms and the community of Round Rock in Arizona.
Tsé Nináhálééh	Bird Monster
Tsés'ná	Wasp People
Tsé Yót'ááhí'áii	Four Pillars of Rocks
Tsézhin Dits'in	Tsaile Butte, Chuska Mountains, New Mexico
Tsin Béél'áhí	Tree Grove Slope (Bill Williams Mountains)
Tsin Biłdeez'á	Wooded Mesa
Tsoodził	Blue Bead or Turquoise Mountain — Mount Taylor

Stinking Lake, El Vado, New Mexico   Tó Niłchoní

Carrizo Mountains in Arizona   Dził Náhooziłii

Glossary

Wíineeshch'įįdii	Locust (Cicada)
Wólázhiní	Black Ants
Wólázhiní Dine'é	"Insect" Beings
Wóóshiyishí	Measuring Worm
Yaa' Hastiih	Lice Man
Yé'ii	God
Yé'iitsoh	Giant (Big Monster)
Yé'iitsoh Bidił	Yei Tso's Blood, south of Mt. Taylor, New Mexico
Yé'iitsoh Łá'í Naagháii	One Walking Giant
Yoołgai Asdzą́ą́	White Shell Woman
Yoołgai Ashkii	White Shell Boy
Yoołgai gish	White shell cane
Yoo' Tsoh	Fortified Mesa, eastern side of San Mateo Mountains in New Mexico

The Fingers, near Chilchinbito, Arizona   *Tsé'íí'áhá*

Waterless Mountain, near Fish Point, Arizona   Tó ádin Dah Azká

Sheep Hill (Mountain), near Flagstaff, Arizona   Dibé Shijé'é

White House Ruin, Canyon de Chelly, Arizona   Kinii' Na'ígai   (according to "Night Chant")

Window Rock, at capital of Navajo Nation, Window Rock, Arizona   Tségháhoodzání